VERMONT WILD

Adventures of Fish & Game Wardens

VOLUME 3

VERMONT WILD

Adventures of Fish & Game Wardens

VOLUME 3

Written by **Megan Price**

Illustrated by **Bob Lutz**

Pine Marten Press

Pine Marten Press

Second edition

Copyright © 2013 by Megan Price

The author reserves all rights to this material in any and all media, whether now known or hereafter devised, and in any form, whether now known or hereafter devised, including, but not limited to: ebooks, magazines, CDs, DVDs, any and all computer and communication services including the Internet, throughout the universe and in perpetuity. Amen.

No part of this book may be reproduced or transmitted in any form or by any means, electronic or mechanical, including photocopying, recording or by any information storage and retrieval method, without written permission from the publisher, except for the inclusion of brief quotations in glowing reviews that will help us sell more books.

Front cover and book design by Carrie Cook.

Printed in the USA

For information and book orders, visit our website:
www.PineMartenPress.com

ISBN: 978-09828872-3-3

Library of Congress Control Number: 2012915183

Answers to your most pressing questions:

Did the stories in this book really happen?
A cougar attack? A snowmobile stuck atop a pine tree?
Monkeys loading rifles? Red and Smokey?
Trust me, I ain't clever enough to make this stuff up!

Have some stories been embroidered just a little?
A whole lot less than, "The one that got away!"

What about the characters?
The wardens are real. Deputy wardens and innocent
bystanders names are used if they have a sense of
humor and swear they won't sue us.

What about the poachers?
We change their names and some of the particulars
so's not to further embarrass their families.
Scofflaws' shenanigans and convictions are real!

Get ready, here it comes....

Big Legalese Disclaimer
Any resemblance to any individual,
living or dead, is one heck of a coincidence.

That's our story and we're sticking to it.

Dedication

This book is dedicated to **Jean**
with gratitude for her
endless enthusiasm,
encouragement,
hard work, patience and
countless acts of kindness.

Without Jean, these books
would never have been written.

And

to all who work to protect
wildlife and wild places.

For more books by Megan Price, visit:

www.PineMartenPress.com

STORIES

"I was sweating despite the −20 degrees and cringing with each swing, expecting to hear a big KA POW any second, signaling the demise of that brand new engine."

TRAIL BLAZER
JINXED

CONTRIBUTED BY JOHN KAPUSTA

I was working in the Rochester area in 1968—deep snows, steep hills and long winters—when the Department decided to take the plunge and buy snowmobiles for a few of us wardens.

At the time, we mostly used wooden snowshoes to get around the woods in winter.

So, when I got the call saying I was assigned a new snowmobile, I was thrilled.

In retrospect, maybe I should have thought of myself more as a guinea pig.

I'm pretty sure my machine was jinxed.

I was looking forward to an end to frozen feet inside soggy, wet boots, walking on turkey platters with leather bindings that stretched, broke and often fell off, long hikes up and down mountains fighting aching thigh muscles and cramped calves.

The promise that I could just yank on a cord, fire up an engine, climb aboard and travel for miles up in the backcountry was very appealing.

Like sitting in a motorized easy chair, right?

When the truck backed into my yard with the shiny red hood glinting in the sun, the plastic cover still on the seat, I was as happy as a kid on Christmas with a minibike under the tree.

I helped the driver unload the machine and he handed me two keys, a couple cans of two stroke oil, and a plastic pouch with the owner's manual, before saying goodbye.

As soon as he was out of the yard, I sat down on the seat, grabbed hold of the handlebars and grinned big, thinking of all the places I could go.

After a minute or two of studying the engine, I trotted inside the house, poured myself a big cup of coffee and began poring over the owner's manual.

After an hour, I thought I had a pretty good grasp of how to fuel up, start and steer the machine. I went back outside, mixed up some gas and oil, put it in the tank, and prepared to launch a test run around my yard.

As any old timer will tell you, starting the first snowmobiles was really a job for two people.

You needed someone to adjust the choke, someone to feather the throttle and someone to pull the recoil starter rope. That's three hands, not two.

Anything less and you had to have the speed and accuracy of a cobra to make it all come together so the machine would keep running.

Like starting a cranky chainsaw at -20 below, the mixture of gas and oil, barometric pressure, angle of the sun, wind speed and direction and the machine's mood were just a few of the critical variables not to be ignored.

Get just one of these wrong and you'd flood the engine, soak the spark plug and be left shaking your head and staring at the machine for hours.

All of this machine moodiness was to become abundantly clear to me later. But for my first ride, I got lucky. After only a dozen or so rotator cuff ripping yanks, she fired right up.

I grinned big, jumped aboard and fiddled with the choke with my left hand, hit the throttle with my right and the machine lunged forward.

I sat down on the seat like in the ads and gave it the gas. The sled leaped forward, propelling me smack dab towards an ancient maple tree.

I quickly realized I couldn't steer worth beans from a sitting position.

So, I jumped up and braced my boots on the running boards and leaned hard left and then hard right and went around and around the yard until I'd made a kind of looping track.

After a half hour of riding, I felt I had pretty much figured this rig out.

With the smile of a conquistador, I rolled up to within 20 feet of my front door and shut her down for the evening. My ears were ringing but that was a small price to pay, I thought.

I went inside the house to put some gear and a travel plan together for exploring the backcountry of my district the next morning. There were deeryards to check, trap lines to follow and more.

Getting to sleep that night was a little tougher than usual, I have to admit.

I was like a kid with his first car. My head was full of all the distant backcountry locations I could travel with this new tool.

The next morning dawned a corker –20 degrees below zero, with a stiff north wind. It was the kind of Vermont morning that turns car batteries into blocks of ice and launches mad searches for jumper cables.

But a little arctic air wasn't going to deter me. I grabbed my snowshoes and my daypack and headed out into the yard to fire up my sled for its very first adventure just after the school bus had picked up the kids.

I was one of the lucky guys who could access miles of woods right out of my yard. My house adjoined Route 100.

I decided to start the machine and let it idle and warm up a bit before I tied my snowshoes and pack to the back with some cotton clothes line.

With the ignorance of a man who believes his initial dumb luck is a sign of only good things ahead, I pulled the choke, pushed hard on the throttle with my right thumb and with my other fist tight on the rope, I yanked on the recoil.

I yanked once, twice and on the third pull, she fired up.

This was going to be a great day.

I took most of the thumb pressure off the gas and looked down at the choke to adjust it. I expected the motor to come back to a nice idle like it had the day before once I got the mixture right.

But the thumb tab didn't snap back and the engine started spinning itself into an eardrum splitting roar.

I took my thumb off the throttle lever entirely, but it made no difference. The engine was winding up more.

I tried jamming a finger behind the lever, to pop it free, but it wouldn't release.

Before I could reach for the ignition key, the track churned and the machine leaped forward like the story of the Morgan stallion, Figure, laying into his traces against a horse three times his size.

I lunged and with my left hand, reached across for the brake lever on the handlebars.

Too little. Too late. No brake was going to stop this steed.

My snowmobile had worked itself into a frenzy like a lit fuse on a Fourth of July bottle rocket. The machine was a'screamin'.

In a big blue fog of gulped gas and oil, she bolted out of my yard like a zebra with a pride of lions on her striped behind.

I ran after her, but I was no match for the dazzling speed of this new engine wound up to warp speed.

My heart was in my throat as my shiny red snowmobile—with less than two miles on the odometer—roared across my lawn, headed straight for busy Route 100.

Out of the corner of my eye I spied a fancy foreign made sedan sporting New Jersey plates and a roof rack loaded with skis.

You know those math problems you were taught as a kid?

The ones about if the Boston train leaves the station at 6 am traveling 50 miles an hour and another train leaves the station at White River Junction at 9 am going 35 miles an hour, when will there be one heck of a big wreck?

Well, I didn't need to be that middle school math whiz to see there was a disaster headed right for me.

I ran waving my arms like a sailor on an aircraft carrier and shouting as loud as I could toward the highway.

The driver never even turned his head my way. He may have thought I was just suffering from cabin fever. But honestly, I don't think he even saw me.

The snowmobile zipped over the snow bank out of my yard and into the highway and missed the car's rear bumper by a hair.

Now for the next lane.

My neighbor, Wilbur Johnson, was a supervisor for the state highway department and took particular pride in building impressive snow banks.

On the opposite side of the road was one of his finest works of the season—a good 10 footer, braced in part by the metal guardrails behind it.

I watched in awe from the side of the road as

my snowmobile zipped across the yellow center line, hit the bank at 40 miles an hour, and smashed through the top two feet of the snow mountain.

It sailed right out of sight.

Now, the national news was full of a possible moon launch during this era.

Seeing my sled sail off into the frosty blue sky was like witnessing a space launch, Rochester style.

My jaw dropped about 10 inches. I looked both ways for traffic, then took off across the highway to see where the snowmobile had landed.

I could hear the engine still running even as I stomped and clawed my way to the top of Wilbur's snow mountain.

I peeked out over the tippy top of the pile and there about 40 feet away from the highway and maybe 20 feet below me is my snowmobile —sitting in the top of a big white pine and spittin' out pine needles and branches like a wood chipper.

If you didn't know better, you would think some nutty loggers had decided to cut a tree down the hard way—starting at the top.

I stood there about three seconds assessing the situation.

Then I turned, slid to the bottom of the snow bank, looked both ways for traffic and ran like crazy for Wilbur's.

His property was a treasure trove of tools. Somewhere near his woodpile, I knew there'd be a hatchet or an ax. Sure enough, under the eaves of his garage I spied a broken peavey and next to it, a rusty ax.

I recognized it as the one Wilbur used for breaking up ice in front of his garage door. It would have to do.

I grabbed it and ran back across the yard, across the highway, up the snow bank, stepped over the top, sat down and slid like a kid to the bottom.

But not before I about scared some poor woman driver almost off the road. It's not every day you see a breathless man in uniform running across the road with a rusty ax in their hand like a lunatic, I guess.

I got to the base of the pine tree with the bent top holding my machine hostage and started swinging that ax, chopping at the trunk as fast as I could.

I was desperate to get the track on the ground before the engine blew.

Of course, Wilbur hadn't sharpened that ax head in many moons. It was slow going. I felt like I was paring a fat carrot with a butter knife.

I managed to make a notch on the low side and then jumped to the high side to drop the tree.

I was sweating despite the −20 degrees and cringing with each swing, expecting to hear a big KA POW any second, signaling the demise of that brand new engine.

I slammed the trunk with the dull blade like a gladiator. Once I worked my way about half way through the tree, the big top began to sway and the heartwood splintered under the weight of the sled.

I jumped back from under the boughs and looked up. I threw the ax aside and slammed my shoulder into the tree like I was busting down a door to a burning apartment.

I pushed and shoved and gritted my teeth until I heard a big crack.

I jumped back and ran for cover. I turned just in time to see the pine fall, in a whooshed "Kuh whump!"

The snowmobile was still screaming, but the skis were hung up in some stout limbs. I leaped and scrambled over the shuddering boughs, dove for the ignition key and twisted it to the off position.

The engine sputtered, gasped and finally died.

I'll save you the details of my chopping limbs
and muscling that sled out of the tree top tangle
and getting it back home.

Other than a few scratches on the hood and
a track that looked like it had traveled 1,000
miles when it had gone less than 600 feet, it
was none the worse for wear—on the outside
anyway.

I couldn't say the same about me. I had
nightmares for a month.

And to prevent the snowmobile from running
away from me again, I took a lesson from an old
friend who logged with a big Percheron team.

"I always point their noses into the side of
a barn when hitchin' my horses," he sagely
advised.

"They might be rarin' to go, but they won't
run through a wall. Well, not most of them
anyway!"

"You'd be riding fast over the snow and hit a
bump, or a breeze would catch that front flap,
and the lid would slam down over your eyes
faster than a roll up window shade
with a broken spring."

Trail Blazer
Snowman

Contributed by Tom Stearns

I was a warden trainee under John Kapusta. John was charged with evaluating me for my suitability to the job not just for my skills, but my ability to think on my feet.

On this particular day, John decided I should take the handlebars of his snowmobile and he'd ride in the back.

We slung our rifles over our shoulders and John hunkered down against what could loosely be called a backrest, put his feet on the rails and settled in.

There were no snowmobile trails. A driver was always breaking trail.

This meant you had to be on constant alert for rocks, cliffs and fallen trees that could tear the machine's skis off and destroy the track.

There was also danger above. Tree branches could take your head off or poke you in the eye. Barbed wire fences were another threat.

You had to take all of this into consideration while going fast enough to make certain the machine didn't bog down in snow. If that happened, it was easy to get stuck and very hard to dig your way out.

It was quite a job muscling these machines around, especially if you didn't know the terrain—which I didn't. The area we were touring was all new ground to me.

I welcomed the opportunity to take the driver's seat, but I was a little nervous. I had no idea where I was going and I certainly didn't want to do any damage to the boss's sled or get us stuck.

I stood up on the boards, hit the throttle and headed out.

I figured I'd keep going until I felt a tug on my trouser leg from John or heard him shout or something.

A good hour passed with me going up and down and around sharp corners through sugarbush and pasture, bumping along deeply rutted logging roads, under pine boughs and through open meadow.

We were looking for sign of dogs chasing deer, back country trappers at remote beaver ponds —basically anyone else nutty enough to be outside when most Vermonters were smart enough to stay huddled next to their wood stoves.

I had on warm mittens—two pairs in fact —
along with long johns, insulated pants and
boots. I was also wearing the Department
issued winter cap, which none of us liked.

I referred to it as "Korean War duck hunter
surplus." Other guys had a lot less flattering
names for these less than stylish head warmers.

The caps were nondescript tan, stuffed with
some mystery bird feathers, sported jaunty little
straps that tied in a bow under your chin like
Mommy would do for you, and a long, flimsy,
floppy brim.

Most of us felt we looked like total dorks
wearing these things. And I am quite certain
many members of the public agreed with us.

You'd stop to talk to someone and you'd see
their eyes drift up to staring at the poofy cap's
ear flaps or the little bow under your chin.

It's not easy trying to assert an air of authority
and professionalism chatting with a veteran ice
fisherman or trapper when they are looking at
your hat and trying not to bust out laughing.

Even worse, these hats posed a real danger.

I have to think the Koreans had maybe
never even heard of snowmobiles at the time
these hats were being sewn. Their duck bill
brims were a real liability when steering a
snowmobile.

You'd be riding fast over the snow and hit a bump, or a breeze would catch that front flap, and the lid would slam down over your eyes faster than a roll up window shade with a broken spring.

When that happened, you were literally driving blind.

If you used your right hand to lift up the lid, your machine would die. You had to keep that thumb pressed hard on the throttle.

That meant you had to use your left hand to lift and hold the bill up to keep from slamming into a tree or going off a cliff. Now, you've lost your ability to steer.

These toppers didn't seem worth the risk to me. But it was part of our official winter uniform, and they did keep my ears warm, so I wore it.

But John wasn't wearing a hat or mittens this day.

Anyhow, after an hour of muscling that machine breaking trail, my back and legs were starting to pinch. I wanted to stop, get off and stretch.

But being the new guy, I also wanted to make a good impression. I didn't want to stop until John told me to.

But after another half hour, my right leg was cramping so bad I didn't have any choice.

I slowed to a stop, hopped off carefully so as not to kick my passenger in the head, bent down to rub my leg, turned and looked at John.

He was plastered from the top of his head to his toes with snow. It looked like I'd taken a snowman for a ride and that snowman was carrying a snowy briefcase on his lap.

I had buried my boss.

For a second, I thought I'd killed him—frozen the man to death. I was speechless.

I forgot all about my kinked up leg, bent down and stammered, "Are, are you all right?"

The snowman blinked, raised his right arm a few inches to shake the snow out of his sleeve, muttered a few choice words and shook his head.

And that's when I found a new use for the duck bill on my hated hat.

I let it fall down over my face to hide my embarrassment.

John drove home.

*"Suddenly, I'm sailing into blue sky and the
engine is screaming like an eggbeater when
you pull it out of the cake mix batter.
My track is catching nothing but air."*

Trail Blazer
Evel Envy

Contributed by John Kapusta

Wardens do get a vacation every now and again and when my neighboring warden took his, it was in deep winter, which is generally the quietest time of year for us.

Still, I got a complaint about dogs chasing deer in his area and headed over to talk to a farmer in Braintree who made the call. I had my snowmobile on the back of a single wide trailer the Department had provided me.

There's a reason those narrow snowmobile trailers aren't much seen anymore. And I am one of the reasons.

I'd had a little incident the previous year, banging over a badly rutted dirt road with lots of "washboard." You know those road ripples that slam your teeth together and destroy your vehicle's suspension.

I managed to keep my truck pointed down the road, but the trailer was a lot lighter, even with the sled aboard.

Like a game of "Snap the Whip" where the folks
at the end of the line get the worst of it, the
cart tires danced like a deer camp cook who
forgot the potholders when he went to pick up a
boiling pot of venison stew.

I watched in horror through my rear view mirror
as the trailer fishtailed toward the ditch and
finally dumped my sled off into the brush.

That little incident resulted in a busted
windshield, a bent ski and left the cowl with a
few more scratches. But it was just a hint of
what was in store for me this trip.

I pulled into the address I was given and found
a thin man with a stubbled gray beard plowing
his yard with a chained up Ford Jubilee tractor.

He shut the tractor off when he saw me, ran
over to my truck and said, "Listen! Do you hear
'em? They been barkin' and yippin' off over in
the back of my land heeah, towards the river
for a couple hours now. Don't sound like no
hounds to me. I think theys a'chasin' deeah."

I stepped out of the truck and listened, too.

I nodded and said, "Mind if I park my truck in
your yard and use this snow machine to go look?"

"No, sir, I sure don't," he said. "Dogs that chase
de-ah, they's likely to be goin' afta my calves come
Spring, don'cha know," he said with conviction.

"Thank you," I said.

I reached back into the cab, grabbed my rifle and ran to the trailer. The snowmobile slid easily off the tilt bed and she fired up on the fourth yank.

With a farewell nod, I punched the throttle lever hard and went roaring off.

I knew I didn't have a lot of time. In deep snow, deer cannot outrun a pack of dogs.

There was bright sun and I was going as fast as the machine could crank, about 40 to 45 miles an hour through a cut field and then onto what appeared to be a woods road.

I slowed a bit entering the forest. The trail in front of me broke into a "Y" 100 feet in, with the right lane looking better traveled.

But I'd heard the dogs off to the left, so I leaned hard to port.

There was bright sunlight ahead. I figured it was another farm field. I punched the throttle as far as she would go.

I was wrong. I was on the lip of the farm's gravel pit.

Suddenly, I'm sailing into blue sky and the engine is screaming like an eggbeater when you pull it out of the cake mix batter. My track is catching nothing but air.

My long flight gave me a few seconds to think

about what was coming and how to land—or try to.

I thought of Evel Knievel, the motorcycle dare devil.

I'd seen TV coverage of a few of Evel's flights. They showed him leaning in over the machine, bending his elbows and holding on tight to the handlebars.

Of course, he was on a motorcycle, not a snowmobile.

But not knowin' what else to do, I figured I'd better try his crouch.

No dice. My sled was heavy in the nose with no springs. It slammed to earth and I went flying—my hands still with a death grip on those handlebars.

In fact, the bar busted right off.

I can't really tell you how much end over end tumbling the sled took as I was doing my own acrobat act—rolling, sliding and spinning like a wheel torn off a race car at Thunder Road.

For once, that duck down doofus hat Tom Stearns told you about came in handy. As I slid along the snow, ice and gravel grating my forehead, that long bill flopped down over my eyes like a turkey's snood.

The flap took the brunt of the ice raspin' rash that my face would have otherwise suffered. It saved me from picking gravel out of my cheeks for weeks.

I ended up in a heap with a mouth full of snow.
I staggered to my feet and went looking for my
machine.

She was a twisted mess.

Despite being a little dazed, the sound of dogs
barking was louder.

I found my rifle in the snow. The sling had
done a good job of stretching my neck about
six inches before we separated in the crash.

I picked up the weapon and trotted through the
woods towards the barking.

Three dogs had a desperate deer surrounded in
a brook.

I did the distasteful job I had to do, and then I
walked back to the gravel pit and picked up as
many parts as I could find and piled them up
on the snowmobile's engine and frame.

There was no quick fix this time. It was
clear to me I needed some sort of snowmobile
wrecker.

I walked the half mile back to the farm on top
of the trail I'd just blazed. I caught up with the
farmer as he stepped out of the milking parlor
and explained my situation.

He shook his head and said, "Geezum, I feel bad
I didn't tell you about the pit. I just figured you
knew it was there."

When I asked for suggestions on getting my
machine out of the woods, he had a tried and
true solution.

"Bess and Buck are the best for gettin' into
the woods and pullin' most anything out," he
explained. "I've been lookin' for a reason to
hitch them hahses. We'll get that machine out
with my stone boat. Don't you worry none,
Warden. You stop back here around this same
time tomorrow mornin' and we'll have her out."

"You sure I can't stay and help?" I asked him.

"Nah, I got barn chores to do first. You go on
home. You might oughtta think about lookin'
yerself over. That was quite a tumble you took
by the looks of you."

I realized then my jacket had a couple of
good three corner tears and my hat was losing
feathers faster than a sick chicken.

I thanked him, unhitched my trailer from my
truck and rolled it back out of the way.

True to his word, when I swung back by the
farm the next morning, I found my trailer piled
high with the remnants of my snowmobile.
It wasn't pretty.

The skis were bent, the fiberglass cowl was
smashed, the windshield and tail light were
shattered. Even the metal back rest was
crunched—leading me to believe the machine

had flipped end over end more than a few times.

I shook my head. It was gonna take a lot of parts to rebuild it, no doubt about it.

I'd brought a tarp with me to discourage parts from flying off as I drove it home, and to hide the damage from prying eyes. Some folks might wonder what a warden was doing with a snow machine in that condition.

I was just about done snugging the load down into a neat little package, when the farmer appeared.

"Good mornin'!" he shouted out before walking over to check on me.

When he got closer he looked at me sideways and said, "From what I seen in my pit, I'd say you're durn lucky to have walked away from that one. T'ain't much left of this heeah snow machine."

"Oh, I'll get her goin' again," I said with stubborn confidence. "I just need to get a few new parts."

"If you say so," he said, shaking his head at me. "Me, I'll stick with my hahses. They don't nevah need any new pahts," he grinned.

*"I'm out in the yard, my eye is tearing up
and hurts bad, my ears are ringing,
my eyebrows are gone."*

TRAIL BLAZER
CREAM PUFF

CONTRIBUTED BY JOHN KAPUSTA

I don't know if it was embarrassment or stubbornness or frugal Yankee genetics or a combination of all of the above, but I was bound and determined not to let that snow machine get the best of me.

I was going to keep it running and I would fix it myself.

I called the dealer and ordered a shop manual —same as the mechanics used to figure out how to repair these machines—and while I soaked in a scalding tub with Epsom salts trying to fade my bruises from that gravel pit wreck, I made a list of all the parts I needed to rebuild it.

It took a half dozen more visits to the dealer over a couple months to do it.

In the meantime, it was back to my snowshoes. I have to say I enjoyed checking trappers' sets the old fashioned way, close up conversations with chickadees and being free of carrying spark plugs, belts, springs and extra gas and oil.

She was back together just in time for the ice to melt. I'd be all ready for next winter.

In fact, when the snow came the following November, she was running so good, I sorta forgot about our checkered past.

I felt like we'd formed a bond—or at least come to an understanding. I was the boss and it was going to do what I asked.

But this little red tiger wasn't done with me yet.

I decided one fine January day that I should adjust the snowmobile's track. I'd been hearing it kinda thumping, a sure indication it was a little loose.

I went next door and asked my friend and neighbor, George Symonds, if I could use his small combination garage, tool shed and repair shop, to do the job.

There wasn't a lot of room in this building.

But George had a woodstove in there and he, or someone before him, had poured a concrete floor.

As best I understood it, George had dropped out of school around 6th grade and went into the woods logging for others until he could save enough money to strike out on his own.

I don't know if he ever learned to read or write

very well, but he sure was handy in the woods and could figure most any piece of equipment out.

Take, for instance, how George managed to get into his workshop to tinker with his crawler when a hydraulic hose needed replacing, track needed bushings or the like.

This was before factory made cages were installed to protect the operator.

George knew a deadfall, or a roll over in the woods could kill him.

So he designed and welded up his own Roll Over Protective Structure—ROPS—for safety.

But George's ROPS was different than any I'd ever seen.

Instead of a squared off canopy, George built his in the shape of a Volkswagen Beetle roof—a seamless sloping arc, like an egg cut in half on the long line.

You see, the crawler's canopy was a good foot taller than the garage door opening.

Weren't no way George could work on his machine inside his shed unless he ripped out the header above the door and replaced it.

That would require a lot of work, as well as lengthening the shed doors and maybe all that extra wood weight would require him to add a third hinge on each door and rehang them, too.

Anyway you figure it, it was going to be a lot of work, time and some money.

But George was a man who thought outside the box—or in this case, his shed.

Like a lot of old outbuildings, the sills sat on laid up fieldstone.

There was no block or poured concrete foundation or nuts and bolts holding them together.

George used what many would consider a flaw to his advantage.

He built that egghead canopy.

And whenever he wanted to get his crawler inside the shop, he pulled up tight to his too low door until the ROPS was just kissing the header.

Then he shifted the crawler in low as she will go gear, and gave the throttle the lightest punt.

His egg shaped canopy would slide right under the header, lifting the entire front end of the garage off its foundation as he rolled the machine forward on its tracks.

Then as the egg top got lower, the shed walls set down again on the fieldstone.

Oh, it would rattle the rakes, shovels and chains hanging on his barn walls a little—kinda like there was an earthquake going on—but that was useful, too.

It shook the cobwebs and dust off his tools.

When George was done replacing the pads or any other repair, he just backed out slowly the same way, and the front of the building would rise up again and then drop back down once he got the nose clear.

Like I said, George was a very smart man.

This day, George had been working inside the shed earlier on some of his projects.

He had the wood stove going.

Not only would I have a hoist, a roof over my head and a dry floor, I'd have heat and tools, too.

For a guy who was used to lying on his back in the woods to work on this machine, George's shed was heaven.

"That's fine, John," George said. "I'm headed into the house to get some lunch."

I thanked him and fired up the sled and rode

her into the garage and pulled the doors shut,
but didn't latch 'em behind me.

I put the hook from the chain lift on the rear
bumper and pulled up the sled.

Then I went to check on the wood stove.
The heat would melt the snow off the tracks
and make my job easier.

I opened the door and saw the fire was low, so
I reached into the woodpile and tossed in a few
sticks of ash and maple.

The stove spit out some embers at my feet as
I shut the door. I didn't think anything of it.
They'd burn out on the concrete floor.

My sled was already dripping a lot of melting
snow onto the concrete from the heat.

I walked over to the tool bench to locate a
wrench to adjust the track.

There was a deer hanging in the shed off to the
side. It was evidence in a pending case. George
had let me store the carcass there as well. I
had to duck between her front hooves as I
searched for the right tools.

I was humming a little tune and feeling quite
sprightly.

George had a simple but sweet set up here and I
sure was lucky to have such a nice neighbor.

I picked up a couple wrenches, turned and had just taken a step towards the snow machine's bumper when it happened.

A blinding flash—strong enough to blow the shed doors wide open, pick me up and throw me 10 feet out into the yard.

The hanging deer slammed me with a hoof as I blew past—caught me right in the eye.

I'm out in the cold, my eye is tearing up and hurts bad, my ears are ringing, my eyebrows are gone.

I'm still holding a wrench.

I look back towards the shed with my one good eye and see flames shooting up from the concrete floor to the ceiling.

I start screaming for GEORGE! and run to save the shed.

I needed water.

But with the temperature hovering around zero this balmy day, the frozen stuff would have to do.

I bent over and started picking up handfuls of snow and throwing them at the flames.

George came running out of his house with half a sandwich in his left hand and a pooched out cheek that made him look like a chipmunk with a stash of hazelnuts.

He took one look at the bright red flames licking up the front of his garage and threw his sandwich down, spit out his wad of Wonder Bread and sandwich meat and came running to help me.

The pair of us grab fistfuls of snow from beside the driveway and throw it at the fire, which did not seem too impressed by our efforts.

Most of the snow evaporates before it even hits the concrete floor.

My right eyelid is swelling shut from the hoof hit.

I cock my head like a rooster looking for June bugs and dart about trying to find chunks of snow to toss into the fire.

I get my hands on a few basketball size chunks of compacted snow and ice, and lob them onto the shed floor like snow bombs.

It helps.

George grabs a metal trash can out behind the garage, dumps out the metal waste inside, bends down and scrapes the nose of the can along the yard like a big Hoover.

Then he leaps and tosses the bucket of snow
at the fire.

It knocks the flames down by half.

He makes another run as I keep lobbing
chunks from just outside the shed door onto
the flames.

In a few minutes, we have the fire out.

I jump inside the shed to drop the sled from
the chain hoist and wrestle it out of the garage,
just in case there might be a second round
waiting for me.

Smoke is wafting up off the snowmobile's front
end.

The nearly new windshield from the gravel
pit incident two years earlier is twisted into a
smoke stained, lumpy mess.

The smell of melted plastic and wiring hits me
in the face as I gingerly lift the hood and look.

My right eye is streaming tears. I'm an injured
Cyclops trying to diagnose an engine problem.

George is beside me.

We study the motor and there it is—a wet spot
running down the side of the gas tank, just
below the seam.

Now, I know what happened.

When I lifted up the back bumper, the fuel inside the tank sloshed forward.

I didn't know it, but the gas tank seam was leaking. The fuel dribbled down and onto the concrete floor.

What I thought was just melting snow was actually a mixture of melting snow with a slick of gas and oil floating on top. When the fuel slick ran into a burning ember from the woodstove, it caused a flashback.

So much for a simple track adjustment today. My snowmobile was seriously out of commission once again.

I shook my head and picked up a broom to sweep out the garage floor.

George looked around inside his garage briefly. Despite the impressive flames, the building wasn't damaged.

He looked at me, saw my eyelid swelling shut like I'd just gone a round with Joe Frazier, and said, "Nice shiner."

Then George walked back to the back door of his house, stooped to pick up the half of his sandwich he had tossed into the snow, blew the snow off it, took a bite, and went back indoors.

I dragged my sled to where it wouldn't be in the
way and then I went to my house and put some
ice on my prizefighter eye.

For the next week, when folks asked, "What
happened?" I told them the truth—I got
punched in the eye by a dead deer.

Before the week was out, I was back at
the dealers ordering more parts: gas tank,
windshield and wiring harness topped the list.

In another week, I had the machine back in the
woods and running good.

I ran that red sled a total of six winters.

Well, if you count the months it actually ran, it
was maybe half the time. I guess it would be
more honest to say I had the machine in my
possession a total of six years.

Not a single day bore any resemblance
whatsoever to the commercials on TV that
promised users effortless fun.

On the other hand, the promise of thrilling
adventure was certainly true—just not the kind
of fun adventure you expected to have.

Looking back, this machine seemed to have a
mind of its own and an agenda straight out of a
horror movie.

Even so, when I got the call ordering me to haul

it over to the Barre Montpelier Road, to
be sold at the annual state auction, I wasn't
sure I wanted to let her go.

It wasn't so much that I wanted to keep it.
I just wasn't sure it was fair to unleash
what may be a cursed sled on some poor
unsuspecting bidder.

But I did what I was told.

And when I pulled up to consign it, the fellows
cataloging items for the upcoming auction were
some impressed.

One of the fellows whistled as he looked the
machine over and said, "Hey, this sled looks to
be in pretty good shape there, Warden!"

He picked up his clipboard and a pen and
asked, "What do you want me to say about her?
Cream Puff?"

"Ha!" I laughed, almost choking. "I wouldn't go
so far as to say that. Uh....why don't you just
write down, 'Many new parts.' "

I handed him the keys as two other fellows
tugged on the bumper to unload it.

I turned to go and felt my coat brush across
something sticking up out of my back pocket.

I'd almost forgotten.

"Oh! Here's the owner's manual for it. And I've got the shop book for the machine here, too," I said, running to get it out of my truck.

I handed both to the fellow with the clipboard. He was busy writing down the model and serial numbers for the auction.

He paused, looked up at me and I told him, "You make sure you sell this machine with these manuals, okay? Because whoever buys this sled is sure gonna need 'em."

No sirree, they don't make snowmobiles like that anymore.

"The beaver twists and rocks until his head slams into my leg—and when he does, he sinks his big orange fangs into my wrinkled waders."

BEAVER BATTLES
FULL HOUSE

CONTRIBUTED BY WAYNE ROWELL

Before the ski areas showed up, the vast acreage between Bennington and Brattleboro was thinly populated logging country. More than a half century later, I guess many would argue not much has changed.

Steep hills, thick woods, cattail filled swamps; black fly clouds in summer and chest deep snow in winter—this land that connects Bennington and Brattleboro is tough on wannabe homesteaders.

Many pioneers with high hopes of taming this forest and scratching a living out of the soil have been forced to admit defeat and move on. There are whole towns that have pretty much been abandoned: Glastenbury, Somerset and Halifax aren't much more than names on a map. Only the hardiest folks live in these towns.

You'd think with all that room to roam humans and wildlife wouldn't bump heads. But often we're not the only ones to look at a piece of land and want to call it home.

And while most wild animals will leave when they come into conflict with humans, beavers are a particularly stubborn bunch.

Convincing a beaver to scrap his blueprints for flooding your land is like telling a squirrel to stop gathering nuts.

Battling beavers can turn into a steady job. You knock holes in their dam in the morning and in a day or two—sometimes even overnight—they've got the hole plugged and you are right back where you started.

Often, just getting to where they've set up shop is an issue. Their lodges and dams are surrounded by water like a good English castle.

It's an often perilous tight rope walk over sharpened saplings and tail daubed mud. Fall and you can easily impale yourself. Almost as bad is the smell.

Beaver stink. Like a lot of wild animals, these critters leave a scent—and while it won't burn your eyes and nostrils like a skunk's perfume will—it can certainly make you gag.

I understand the most expensive perfumes use the oil from beavers' musk glands as a base.

I have to think that if some of those models got a whiff of that musk in its original state or took a close look at where that expensive man catching odor originated—under a beaver's tail—many would run screaming to the powder room to upchuck their lettuce leaf lunch.

But back to my story.

I had a number of clashes with beavers over the years. My goal was always to relocate them. But that was seldom easy because they're a stubborn bunch.

One of my most memorable adventures occurred when I assisted a respected Woodford sawyer by the name of George Bugbee.

George ran what was probably the last operating water powered sawmill in the state. That mill along a spur of the Roaring Branch River had been in his family since 1866, according to the history books.

I don't know what generation George was in the line of Bugbee men operating the mill, but sadly, he was the last.

Paved roads and more reliable cars and trucks meant folks could buy kiln dried lumber and even have it delivered to their door.

Unlike those skinny store bought sticks that are stamped with blue dye like a side of beef, Bugbee lumber was never stamped and so it's about impossible to say where the framing of the old homes in this area came from 200 years ago.

But I have to believe many of the square roofs

you see in the old clapboard houses and
barns for 10 or more miles in all directions
surrounding Woodford were sawn at Bugbee's
mill by generations of Bugbees.

But running water attracts beavers like a dinner
bell. And that's what it did here.

And that's why I got a call from my neighboring
warden over in Woodford, telling me that George
was having a problem with beavers.

Would I mind helping George out?

Woodford wasn't part of my district, but my pal
knew I didn't mind dealing with the critters.

Beavers had found the Bugbee Mill tail race
—the pond just below the mill—inviting.

It wasn't long before they had their own logging
operation going over at George's place.

They were dropping trees and saplings
from the banks of the Roaring Branch River
and having a grand old time slapping together
a community in the catch pond below the
mill's water wheel.

If the toothy rodents were allowed to continue,
they would back up the water enough to stop
George's waterwheel dead, and maybe even
flood him out.

I loaded my waders into my truck along with a

couple empty grain bags and headed out bright and early the next morning.

I parked near the mill just off Route 9 and picked up my binoculars and strolled over to the bank. I made several slow passes looking for signs of the troublemakers.

Sure enough, I saw beaver chewed stumps on the opposite bank and dozens of saplings laid crossways at the spillway.

It wasn't but five minutes later George strolled over and together we came up with a plan of attack.

I'd go down into the water with my waders on with George as my assistant. Together, we'd get the rascals into separate grain bags and tie the bags shut. Then I'd lay the sacks in the back of my truck and drive 'em on up into Somerset where the animals would have a good long walk back. That should discourage them from returning.

While I don't recommend you try this at home, with patience and practice you can catch beavers by grabbing them just in front of their tails and dropping them into a sack.

They don't like it and they'll squirm and try to bite you, of course.

It's a bit like grabbing onto a rattlesnake—except beavers weigh 10 to 40 pounds, are soaking wet and digging at you with their stubby legs and impressive claws and looking to sink their ugly orange teeth into your hide.

Maybe snagging a rattlesnake would be easier?

The wading chase and grab plan works best with the young ones.

Any beaver can inflict a very nasty bite—just ask a tree. Wrestle with an adult beaver with kits it wants to protect and you are really asking for a fight.

My tool of choice for beaver relocating was my bare hands and a potato fork purchased from Montgomery Ward. With an ash handle and prongs, it had just the right heft and strength to tackle several aspects of this unique job.

First and foremost, I could use it as a walking stick to help me get down steep banks and into the water.

Secondly, the hooks help pry beaver dams and houses apart—stick by stick.

And lastly, I used the back of the fork to stun swimming beavers.

I'd tap them on the back of the head with it— just hard enough to stun them. Then I'd bend down, grab their tails and drop them into a sack.

And that was the plan I intended to use today.

"How you going to get on top of them?" George asked.

"You're going to step on top of their lodge and do a little dance. When they come shooting out to investigate, I'll snag 'em," I grinned.

George's eyebrows shot up and he looked slightly skeptical. But he stopped short of telling me I was nuts.

"Let me go get my waders," he said. "I'll be right back."

I went to my truck, pulled on my waders, stuffed a couple burlap sacks between my shirt and bib and picked up my potato hook.

Then I started into the shallow man made pond with George following.

I strolled quietly into the mill's water. I didn't want to make a wake or speak or do anything that might spook them. When beavers get scared, they slap the water with their tail to warn the others before diving and swimming to safety—most of the time. Rarely, they have been known to attack.

Odds were they'd been busy on the night shift and were inside their lodge asleep. I was hoping if they were out working, they'd think of us as nothing more than big rubber legged shore birds looking for a fish dinner. But if the animals saw us a threat, we could be in trouble.

Biologists claim beavers' long orange incisors grow as much as four feet a year. How they ever measured that is anyone's guess. But anyone who has studied the beasts realizes they live to chew and chew to live. A beaver can gnaw a five inch thick willow tree clean through in three minutes. While a willow is about as soft as softwood trees go, that's still pretty impressive.

I mean, I wonder how long it would take you to chomp through a willow?

Compare beavers daily chow downs to a human's all you can eat contests and it makes our species look pretty puny.

When it comes to gnawing, rodents rule, and beavers are at the top of the North American rodent class.

Which is why I didn't want any part of my body anywhere near those long pumpkin colored teeth.

I could walk in my chest waders while keeping an eye out for any ripples in the pond or bubbles rising to the surface—signs the beavers were on the move.

Beavers aren't the fastest swimmers, clocked at maybe five miles an hour. But compared to a warden in waders, that was more than fast enough. I knew I'd only get one chance.

It only took us a couple minutes to slide up to

the side of the beaver lodge. I gave George a
hand so he could make his way up to the top
of their home, even as I was searching for their
front door.

Beaver lodges' entrances are always under
water.

When I found the entrance, I laid my fork down
on top of the lodge not far from George's feet.
I wanted to have it at the ready, but hoped I
wouldn't need it.

Then I pulled a sack out of my bib, handed it
to George and whispered to him it was time to,
"Start dancin'!"

Well, George gets his elbows up like he's
about to the do the Chicken Dance at a Polish
wedding reception and he purses his lips
like this is serious business and he starts in
stomping like a champion clogger.

The first beaver pokes his head out and I strike
like a cobra as he begins his slide out the lodge
door into the water.

I grab the animal by his tail and lift him up
high. He's a nice youngster, a good 10 pounds
or more.

George has the burlap bag open wide and
his eyes and mouth about match the bag's
opening as he moves it far out in front of him
trying to catch the water rat, who's clawing at

the air wondering what just happened.

I slide the critter inside the bag and George crushes the fabric together with his big hands and starts to knot it up.

I warn George, "Keep that bag away from your body, just in case he decides to chew his way out!"

George jumps back so far he about tumbles off the lodge roof and drops the bag beside his boots, the top tied. His arms are way out in front of him as I hand him another burlap sack.

I see ripples forming in the water below me again and I elbow George, "Here comes another one!"

George scrambles to open the second grain bag and I bend down and strike again with my right hand.

I nab number two and while he's heavier than the first one, he doesn't seem to have as much fight in him.

George is ready and grins big as we bag beaver number two. We are making this look easy.

We get three beavers in a matter of 10 minutes and I'm feeling pretty good about it.

The bags are full and I'm thinking it's time

we head to shore when something catches the corner of my eye. It's another brown head poking up.

Must be a deep sleeper and it takes a lot to wake him up?

"Holy Smokes! It's another one, George!" I shout. "Get ready!"

I reach into my bib and feel around and realize we've used up all the burlap sacks.

"I'm outta bags! Open one up quick," I say to George.

I know if we don't get all the beavers out of here at once, the one we leave behind will just start damming the pond up all over again, even without his friends.

George bends down and tries to loosen the knot on a bag where a thrashing beaver is already trying to bust out.

It's a delicate maneuver to try and untie the knot and not get bit doing it and George has big working man hands.

I stab through the water at the brown flash coming out of the lodge entrance and clamp my fingers hard and fast around a piece of the animal.

I quickly realize this ain't no baby beaver. It's

the difference between a garden snake and a
20 foot Anaconda—an Anaconda with teeth and
claws.

"I got him, George! Open 'er up!" I groan,
pulling up hard and turning towards the sawyer
with a very angry 30 pound beaver in my grip.

The slippery rodent is twisting and thrashing
and chattering. He's a furry cranked chainsaw.

George is taking my earlier advice about
standing back.

He's having trouble leaning forward with
the bag while boosting his backside to
the breeze and trying to help me
net this giant rodent.

The water rat is swinging from side to side like
a crazed pendulum. George is swaying below
with the open burlap sack but just a lick outta
sync.

The beaver twists and rocks until his head
slams into my leg—and when he does, he sinks
his big orange fangs into my wrinkled waders.

"Yeeee-ow!" I yelp.

"Come on, George! Open the sack wider!"
I shout. "Wider!!"

George lines up the mouth of the burlap bag
and I drop the beaver inside.

Done.

But apparently sharing a lodge is one thing,
and sharing a sack is another when it comes to
beavers.

Or maybe these two just had a grudge against
one another. I'll never know.

But I'd no more than dropped beaver number
four into the bag with beaver number three
when all Hell breaks loose.

Tails slapping, teeth chattering, fur flying and
claws clambering—a beaver blow out.

It was as if someone had thrown ice into a
blender and hit the ON button without the lid on.

Poor George is trying to close up the burlap
bag with better than 50 pounds of riled rodents
rolling and ripping inside.

I quickly reach into a pocket for some twine
to tie the bag, hoping the dark will calm the
critters down.

But it's like trying to wrap a cord around an
unbalanced washing machine on the spin cycle.

The beavers, George and I—we're all being
thrashed silly by the fury inside the sack.

Suddenly, there's an explosion and a beaver
dives up and out of the bag, slams me in the

chest and its mud flap tail smacks me in
the face.

The furious rat does a back flip, lands on the
lodge and slides into the pond.

I'm sure not going to make another grab for
him. I want to keep my fingers.

George lifts up the bag, which is a lot lighter
now that the giant has bolted. We carefully peer
inside.

There's one beaver left, hunkered down in
terror. His hands are up to his face covering his
eyes. I think he's praying.

I don't blame him. I am, too. That was a close
one.

I straighten my back and when I do, my right
boot slips out from under me.

Now, I'm teetering on top of the beaver lodge,
bent over backwards with my arms twirling
like I'm a kid playing helicopter—about to fall
backwards into the pond.

George reaches over and grabs one of my
suspenders and pulls hard. I throw myself
forward and get my footing again.

Once I'm standing square, I scan the pond for
signs of the escaped beaver.

George spots her first. "There!" he says, pointing to the mill's foundation.

George and I watch open mouthed as the beaver clambers through an opening in the stones there.

Like the story of the Three Little Pigs, I guess she's decided stone beats sticks and daub and she's going for a bigger, stronger house to get away from these crazy rubber legged wolves.

George looks at me with raised eyebrows as if to say, "Now what?"

"Don't worry, George," I say. "I've got a live trap in my truck. We'll get it later. But let's get these animals out of here before the sun gets high."

George and I wade back through the catch pond to my truck with the bagged beavers.

That's when I notice a hole in my waders.

I'm listing to one side like a sinking ship. By the time I hit the millpond's bank, I'm walking like a fat man in quicksand.

It takes some effort to pull myself up onto dry land.

Once I get to the truck, I see a three inch gash in my waders about half way between my knee and ankle.

It's time to shimmy out of my leaky rubber suit and check the damage to my hide.

I peel off the waders and find a neatly edged, egg shaped hole—the length of a dollar bill in my pant leg.

There's only one layer left and that's my hide.

I throw my dripping wet leg up onto the tailgate, roll up the cuff and inspect the next layer—me—with George nearby.

There's a deep scrape down my shin maybe four inches long. But it's clear my waders and trousers took the brunt of the bite.

George steps in, bends close and studies my shin for a couple seconds, then rights himself and gives his assessment.

"Lucky," he says.

"Gotta be in this job, George," I laugh, "and yours, too, or we wouldn't last long!"

I drove the bagged beavers over to a remote pond a good distance away and let them go.

All three waddled off looking healthy—even the little one who looked like he'd been saying his prayers earlier.

And within two days, George and I managed to catch the big beaver in a live trap. I drove her over to the same spot to keep the family unit together.

A bicycle tube repair kit patched my waders.

My beaver bit shin healed over time, although it left a mark. But you know, that wasn't such a bad thing.

Pulling on my socks some mornings I'd see that scar, think of George Bugbee and our beaver battle, shake my head and chuckle.

Not a bad way to start your day, you know?

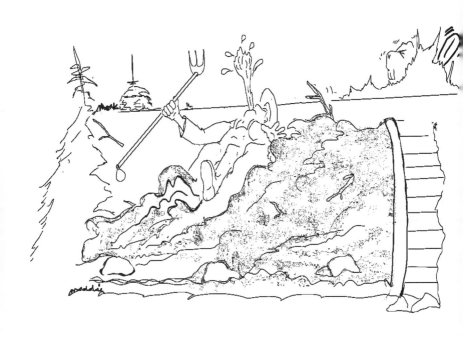

*"I had a face full of beaver mud, filthy frayed
sticks and water soaked bark rushing at me,
making their way into my ears, nose and
mouth—trying to choke me to death."*

BEAVER BATTLES
STRAIGHT FLUSH

CONTRIBUTED BY WAYNE ROWELL

I don't know if beavers hold a grudge or complain about us humans among themselves, but a little more than a year later, some cousins of the Bugbee Mill Pond beavers had a good laugh at my expense.

It started off innocently enough.

I was bumping along in my truck way out in the woods of Halifax along a private road when I spotted a problem.

Water was backing up in a culvert that ran beneath this single track access to the owner's remote seasonal home.

All wardens strive to have good relationships with private landowners in their area.

It's a benefit to the warden to be able to access large tracts of land in all seasons to check hunters' and anglers' licenses and perform other aspects of our jobs.

And for the landowner, a warden provides another trusted pair of eyes and ears checking on their property.

With deer rifle season a few weeks away, I wanted the benefit of driving this old woods road during my busiest time of year. It would save me a couple miles of walking to a popular deer hunting spot.

So, in these situations, I was a one man road crew. If I found a tree had fallen across the road, I moved it. And checking culverts running under the road was important, too.

In these mountains, storms come up often and a downpour can race down a mountain into a clogged culvert and take out entire roads in a matter of minutes.

"Gully washers" we call 'em.

They talk about a stitch in time saves nine? Well, cleaning out a clogged culvert is the same idea.

I always carried a pick and shovel in the back of my truck, along with my hip waders and my potato fork just for these occasions.

Using leverage and elbow grease I could generally free up the rocks, sticks and mud that would collect in these big drain pipes.

It just takes time and a willingness to get your

hands dirty and maybe crawl on your belly through a swamp.

The public mostly sees us in spotless uniforms, but the truth is being a warden often means getting your hands dirty, your feet wet and your back sore.

The fact I'd spent a decade as a dairy farmer in Tunbridge before I signed on as a warden gave me the right attitude, I think.

Nothing like milking cows twice a day seven days a week and endless chores to make a person feel comfortable up close and personal with mud and manure.

I stopped my truck, jumped out and saw this culvert had a big problem.

Water was pooled up on the high side, blocked by a series of downed trees that acted as a dam, allowing rocks, gravel and mud to pile up behind it. And the majority of the trees had the tell tale points of beavers at work.

If that barrier was allowed to remain in place and we got a hard rain, the road would wash out.

Time to get to work.

I shut off the truck, dug out my patched waders, grabbed my potato fork and scooted down the bank.

A closer look showed me what I really needed
was a backhoe. This blockage had been
building for a while, hidden by the tall reeds.

I muckled on to boulders the size of soccer balls
along with saplings, mountain run gravel and
swampy green mud and tossed it all as far away
from the culvert as I could.

I was at it a good hour and still the water was
backed up.

I decided I'd better have a look at this
stoppage from the opposite side of the pipe.
I hiked over the bank, potato fork in hand,
through cattails and green burdocks and
goldenrod, stirring up swarms of mosquitoes
with each step.

The good news was this end of the pipe was
open. The bad news was, there was no light at
the end of the tunnel looking back, despite my
straining and digging.

I decide to get down on my hands and knees
and crawl inside the culvert to tackle the clog
from this side.

I figured at least this way, I'd be working with
the flow instead of against it—if I ever got the
flow to go.

I heard some scuttling as I crawled inside the
pipe—and it wasn't my paws or claws making
tracks. But as long as I didn't land right on

whatever was upset by my arrival, I knew I'd be all right.

Once inside the culvert, I began clawing and pawing and tugging. The smell wasn't the best, but it was a good 20 degrees cooler inside the pipe and I'd left most of the mosquitoes behind.

I don't know how long I was in there, but just when I'm thinking, "I gotta be close here. Maybe I should back outta here and tackle this from the high side again," I hear a loud crack.

It's coming from inside the tangle right in front of my nose.

The potato hook shivers in my hand and pushes back at me.

Uh oh. I snap my head back to take in the bigger picture.

The pile of mud, rocks and sticks shudders in front of my eyes, like there's a little earthquake somewhere.

My brain attempts to register if what I just saw, I just saw—you know what I mean?

I'd been expecting to see a building trickle of water, giving me plenty of time to wriggle backwards outta the pipe on my elbows and knees.

But Mother Nature has something else in mind.

I hear the sound of rocks and branches scraping across metal—a growing deafening screech—coming right at my nose.

You know that feeling you get just before all Hell breaks loose?

This was one of those.

A chill goes up my spine—or tries to. I don't think it made it outta my shorts before the screech turned into a roar.

I jump to my knees so fast I slam my head on the top of the pipe. I start back pedaling outta that cylinder as fast as I can.

Trouble is some of the sticks and stone and mud I've thrown behind me like a badger digging a hole, are catching on my sleeves and grabbing my trousers.

But not to worry. Mother Nature is about to take care of these little trifles.

I'd skedaddled backwards on my hands and knees maybe four baby strokes when the scraping sound of wood on metal turns into an ear piercing screech.

KUH WOOSH.

I barely have time to shut my mouth and close my eyes.

You know the "all legs straight out, grabbing
for anything to hold onto" that the bug in the
toilet bowl makes when Mom hits the flush
handle on the toilet?

Well, I hate to admit it, but at that moment,
that was me.

I was the bug in the bowl.

My fingernails claw at the wavy washboard
interior of the scoured culvert. Why I thought
I'd want to stay in there, I don't know.

I guess when you feel your body being
tossed and turned and flushed down a pipe
your first instinct is to try and grab ahold of
something—anything.

I had a face full of beaver mud, filthy frayed
sticks and water soaked bark rushing at me,
making their way into my ears, nose and
mouth—trying to choke me to death.

I slam my eyelids shut, take a deep breath,
duck my chin to my chest and start praying.

If some of the stout sticks I'd yanked out of the
blockage got jammed sideways in the pipe, I
might not get out of this deluge alive.

I do my best to turn myself into a football,
hands at my side and slide—hoping to slide
through the mess and not get hung up.

The next thing I know, I'm lying on my back in flattened, water soaked weeds.

I open an eye—as far as I can. My eyelids are coated in a layer of mud like an ancient Hollywood starlet's mascara.

I suck in a breath, sputter and cough. I spit out a few tablespoons of grit and putrid water and consider myself lucky to still be among the living.

I lift my head a couple inches and turn to look behind me. I'm a good eight feet away from the end of the culvert, but I can see daylight out the other side at last.

A little unorthodox, but I got the job done.

I try to bend my knees—but it feels like I've been coated in plaster or concrete.

The water and muck and sticks are jamming my ribs and armpits from all directions—all the way down to my toes.

Every time I move I get poked. I feel like a pincushion at a quilting bee.

I unhook my suspenders and try to wriggle free. I dig, toss mud, stretch, peel the waders lower, then dig and peel again. I half expect a frog or crayfish to jump out.

Once I'm on my feet, I look for my potato hook.
I find it about six feet south of where I landed.

I waddle back to the culvert on squishy felts,
bend down and peer the length of the pipe.
The inside is now as shiny clean and silvery
bright as if someone had gone through it with
a scrub brush.

I climb back up to the road using my potato
hook as a walking stick and carrying my waders
over my other arm.

A rustling in the weeds catches my ear. I look
back over the roadway and see just the backs of
two round brown bodies skittering off into the
brush. Woodchucks? Maybe.

But more likely it was beavers investigating
what had happened to their dam project.
If they were more intelligent animals, I'd almost
think they'd planned this—a kind of beaver
revenge for evicting their cousins over at
Bugbee's sawmill earlier.

But more likely, it's just that some days you're
the plumber and some days you're the plug.

And on this particular day, I was both.

"The hood rider's backside shoots into the air to new heights and the look on his face goes from deep concentration to total terror."

KEEPIN' UP
WITH THE JONESES

CONTRIBUTED BY STAN HOLMQUIST

Every lawman has them—a dirty dozen whose names rise to the top of the suspect list whenever something goes missing: a beat up car or truck is found abandoned by the side of the road or—of most importance to me as a warden—when there's evidence of poaching going on.

Generally, they're not really bad guys—just a few bubbles off plumb in the way they go about doing things. And sometimes it's not just one fellow but an entire family with some peculiar habits.

This is a story of one colorful clan—the Jones family.

I had a number of incidents implicating the Jones boys over the years, sometimes in cooperation with the state police but just as often alone.

Their base of operations was a dilapidated house way up in the hills on a dead end dirt road.

It had been a hired hand's home, part of a bigger hillside farm that had failed maybe 20 or more years earlier. How the Jones family got the rights to it, I could never figure out as I never knew any member of the family to hold down a full time job that would have paid a mortgage and property taxes.

I always suspected it was some sort of squatters' rights situation as opposed to actual ownership—maybe an absentee owner who had given up trying to get them out and was just waiting for the town to condemn the house as unsafe, or for it to just tumble down around them.

The place was a mess by most anyone's standards.

The roof was a patchwork of curling asphalt shingles, blue tarps, torn flashing splashed with buckets of tar and every now and again what looked to be an original piece of sheet metal rusting red with age.

The roofline sloped like a 30 year old swaybacked horse. There were a couple low points where seedlings sprouted.

Clapboards were torn off, others flapped in the breeze. It looked like someone had tried painting the place at least on one side. But they musta run out of paint, energy or both.

Panes in the old six over six wood frame

windows were broken out and patched here
and there with cardboard and duct tape.
In another spot, someone had used flashing
that looked like it had been cut to fit with
a dull ax.

The wooden porch steps sat cockeyed atop
a couple broken concrete blocks, and what
balusters hadn't been kicked out were deeply
scored—having been gnawed on by an endless
series of snarling mutts that served as sentries
against bill collectors and officers of the law,
like me.

The yard was a minefield of rusted car parts,
ancient baby strollers, smashed pieces of red,
blue and yellow plastic toys along with bicycles,
motorcycles and metal appliance cabinets all
rusted and twisted through with grapevine as
big around as a man's wrist.

Now and again, there'd be a pony staked out in
the yard or tethered to a piece of the wreckage.
The pony served a dual role—lawn mower and
transportation.

When the police were after one or more of the
Jones boys for any one of multiple vehicular
infractions or petty thefts, they'd send one of
the kids to town on the pony to pick up supplies
rather than chance an encounter with the law
driving another unregistered, uninspected car
to town with an unlicensed driver at the wheel.

But just until the heat was off, of course.

Then the pony was turned loose to fend for himself. This would result in complaints from neighbors who would find a thin, flea bitten equine greedily eating their lawn, stomping through their vegetable garden, or both.

There were brothers and cousins and sisters and wives and an endless bunch of kids comin' and goin' at all hours under the sagging, tarped roof.

A tough minded matriarch ruled the roost or at least tried to keep a lid on the simmering pot of unending drama that was always bubbling.

The Jones men were skinny, pasty guys with stringy brown hair and an endless collection of faded T shirts and torn jeans, Mullet hair cuts, untied logging boots, perennial bad attitudes and teeth to match.

As run down as the residence was, it had a couple of things in its corner as a preferred hideout for outlaws.

The house sat on a little rise at the end of the dirt road. Any approaching vehicle came into view about 400 feet from the Joneses' front door.

This gave whatever suspects were hiding inside a good start on high tailing it out of the house, into the tall grass, brush and junk surrounding the house. Bent over and scurrying, they could slip up into the large expanse of adjoining woods before the police or warden pulled into the driveway.

It wasn't quite as romantic as ducking behind sagebrush and cactus like in the Western dramas that blared continually on their old console, but it was just as effective.

I had the occasion to visit the Jones residence one fine March morning when three inches of heavy wet snow had fallen the night before.

I'd found evidence of a deer jacking two days earlier and my sources said it was the Jones boys that had done the shooting.

An abandoned car found not far from where I found a fresh deer hide along with boot and sneaker prints made me think my source might just be right.

The Jones clan was famous for buying their vehicles from local junkyards on the cheap, driving them away and never bothering to register or inspect them.

If they put a license plate on the vehicle, it would be expired or "borrowed" from another vehicle.

Driving with expired plates, stolen plates or no plates at all was just how the Jones family rolled—literally. Of course, it was pretty rare for one of the boys to have a valid driver's license, too.

When their salvaged rigs could be driven no more, they just left the vehicles by the side of the road and went back to the junkyard to buy a replacement as soon as they could get more cash together. If they'd bother to put a license plate on it, they took that with them and any trace of their brief ownership.

The empty beer cans, cigarette packs, Twinkie and Slim Jim wrappers stayed.

With no registration, title or any paperwork in the vehicle to trace it to the Joneses, the police weren't able to do much about the rusty carcasses that regularly littered the back roads.

Police might go to a junkyard and say, "Did you sell this car to one of the Jones boys?" And even if the junkyard owner said he had and we went and tracked down the clan member who bought it, he would say he'd sold it to someone else for $50 or it had been stolen out of his yard before he ever got it on the road.

Taxpayers footed the bill for a tow back to the junkyard time and time again.

Of course, these stories didn't work all the time. No lie ever does, right?

Like that March morning when I wanted to have a little talk with Billy Jones.

I'd just pulled into the yard and popped my cruiser door open when I heard a commotion inside the house, 50 feet away. There were yelps and howls and screeches and the sound of chairs being scraped across a wood floor and tables banged around.

Probably 20 to 30 people were in that tiny house and a good third of them were wanted for something or thought they were.

I walked up to the door and knocked and it goes quiet inside the house like a church service about to start and I had just stepped into the pulpit, and was preparing to address the congregation.

Of course, it wouldn't be a church sermon without a squalling baby or two unseen in the background and as soon my knuckles banged on the edge of the screen door that hadn't seen a screen in years, at least three babies began kicking up a fuss somewhere inside.

I had to knock several times, but within five minutes, Mrs. Jones opened the front door.

Whatever sentimentality had been born in that lady's heart a half century before had been stomped into dust a long time ago. She had the steely squint of a gunslinger and a permanent scowl.

I always got the impression she wasn't so much protective of her brood as she just didn't want to be bothered. Her home had become a flophouse for an endless stream of her kids, their kids, their girlfriends, boyfriends and everybody else's kids.

"Hello, Stan," she said, cracking the door a foot. Her voice was dripping with boredom.

"Billy home, Mrs. Jones?" I asked.

"I don't know. Let me check," she says and turns her head two inches to the right and juts her neck and chin out like a cow in search of her calf and bellers, "BILLLLEEEEEE! You here? Warden's here to see youuuuuuuuu."

I make a note to myself to step back a few more paces or bring earplugs with me next time. This lady could shout.

The house goes kinda quiet—except for the bawling babies—and we stand there in silence, awaiting an answer from Billy.

Nothing.

Mrs. Jones turns to glare back at me after a minute or so. Now I hear a cartoon track on a TV, a young mother repeating, "Don't DO that!" and despite the din, even a manly snore or two in the background.

Finally, Mrs. Jones shrugs, shakes her head and says, "I guess he's not here, Stan."

I don't have a warrant with me. And I know from experience that without one, I am not getting in. This isn't the Jones family's first visit from law officers and they are not going to let me in without one.

But you never know what you might see from the outside, and I've driven quite a distance, so I ask, "Mind if I look around outside?"

The lady of the house shrugs her shoulders and says, "Be my guest," and at the same time swings a slippered foot out behind her several inches to the right to push a toddler who is trying to make a break for it, back into the house.

It's a move worthy of a soccer star. She swoops him back inside and without another word, shuts the door in my face.

I make a wide arc around the yard perimeter. Coming in close would be a big mistake—it's a disaster.

I round the corner of the house and I see just why Billy isn't home.

There's a trail of fresh sneaker prints coming out of a broken cellar hatchway that hasn't seen a door on its empty hinges for many years.

The tracks lead to a grove of pine trees and brush about 100 yards parallel to the road I just drove up.

It's pretty clear that while Ma Jones was having

me wait at the front door, Billy—or someone on the run from the law—was making tracks out the back.

I walk over to within six feet of the hatch, lean down and shine my flashlight into the cellar.

There's a sea of black trash bags down in that basement. And despite the snow on the ground, the stench coming out is gag a maggot awful—a combination of dirty diapers, rotting meat and soured milk.

Rather than go to a landfill or trash transfer station the family was just throwing all their garbage into the cellar. There must have been 100 bags of rotting trash down there.

I shake my head. It must be like swimming in a giant box of stinky foam peanuts, holding your breath and clawing your way through this stink to fresh air.

Billy must really not want to see me.

I don't make a big deal out of what I'm seeing. I just walk around the yard a bit more and then stroll over to my cruiser and leave.

I drive down the road out of sight of the house, around a little bend, pull over and walk into the woods to see if I can find his trail.

Sure enough, I find footprints about 200 feet into the woods. And it's clear this isn't the first time this path has been used. I had to give the boys credit. It might not be a pleasant escape route, but it was effective.

I knew I wasn't the only lawman visiting the house on a regular basis and Billy wasn't the only Jones boy that police were routinely interested in questioning when something went missing. I'd be sure to share my findings with the state police—later.

First, I wanted to use what I'd just learned to set my own trap.

I waited a few days and then made the winding drive up the road again to the Jones residence. This time, I had Tom Simpson, a deputy warden, with me. Tom and I had hatched a little plan.

Tom dropped me off down the road out of sight of the Jones residence.

"Wait here five minutes, then drive on up to the house, knock and ask to speak with Billy," I instructed. "Don't try and go in. Just wait outside until they say he isn't home. Then just nod and say you'll try again later, and come on back down and just wait for me here."

Tom winked and drove on up the hill out of sight.

I got out of the cruiser and ducked into the woods, walking until I intersected that boot stomped trail. I found a spot behind a large white pine about five feet off to the side and hid.

Twenty minutes later I hear the sound of sneakers slapping the melting March snow and a guy wheezing and running up the trail towards me.

I take a peek through the green needled branches. I see a fellow in a T shirt, baggy blue sweatpants and sneakers, pumping his scrawny arms for all he's worth, his stringy hair flowing out behind him.

I wait until the runner is within 15 feet of the pine tree, then I jump out, blocking his path.

"Hello, Billy!" I say, with a great big grin on my face.

The poor guy could not have been more surprised if Bigfoot had jumped him.

He slams the brakes on his tennis shoes, skids about 12 feet on his heels with his arms flailing like a ceiling fan in reverse and then falls flat on his arse in the snow and mud at my feet.

He lies there gasping for breath with his arms fluttering—kinda like he was an infant trying to make snow angels. His mouth is open so wide he could swallow a robin's nest whole.

I'm doing all I can not to bust out laughing at him.

I cross my arms and just wait.

After a good minute of gasping for air, he rolls onto his side, brings his knees to his chest and wheezes, "Jeezum Crow, Stan! You about scared me to death!"

When he finally gets his wind back, I offer Billy a hand up and help him get onto his feet.

"How'd you know I was comin' through here?" he wheezes.

I just smile.

"What do you know about a doe shot down on Lion Head Road a week ago, Billy?" I say.

Of course, he denies knowing anything about the doe and claimed he was home that night.

And since none of his friends would agree to testify against him in court, and there were likely five or more relatives in the Jones house that would swear he was home all night on that particular evening—even if he wasn't—I didn't get far on this particular case.

But I had put Billy and his brothers on notice that it was a bad idea to lie and run when I had taken the time to pay them a personal visit.

This little stumble was an indication of a bigger tumble to come a few months later, when

Billy's luck—and that of a brother and cousin—
ran out in a rather spectacular way.

I was staking out a field off Quarry Road
in Rochester this night—a popular spot for
poachers' late night potshots—with the capable
assistance of Deputy Wardens Tom Simpson
and Henry Giddings.

The pair were on patrol in a separate vehicle.
We were in touch by radio.

It was late June. The first haying of the
season had been done, there'd been a couple
nights of warm summer rain. The grass
growing back was a sweet temptation for any
deer. And the return of deer to these hidden
fields was a big temptation to a lot of poachers.

I backed my cruiser into the brush, stepped out
and set my back up against a nice big ash tree
and settled in to watch and listen.

It was around one in the morning when I heard
a vehicle coming at a crawl, its headlights off,
its exhaust purring like an inboard Cris Craft
about to take on passengers at the dock.

Whatever was rolling at me, it needed a new
muffler. And that was kind of unusual,
because poachers generally try to keep their
transportation very quiet.

I look towards the road and see the car's
headlights are off.

When the driver hits the farm trail leading into the hay field, he turns in, ignoring the bright orange and black No Trespassing sign the owner had posted months earlier. Even in the dark, it's clear the land is posted.

As the car slips past me, I peer around the trees to get a closer look, trying to get a license plate, a make of the car or truck and the number of occupants.

But I never get that far. Slipping on by me was a guy on the hood, arms crossed, holding a rifle in his lap.

Had these fellows taken a tip from some National Geographic special on TV and decided to go on safari?

If you had a fancy 4WD Land Rover with the flat hood and hand railing all around, that wouldn't be a bad tactic. But the jalopy this crew was piloting looked more like a dented hay bale with wheels.

The driver stopped, the car lurched slightly and someone in the passenger seat threw a switch on a hand held light and began shining the meadow.

I looked at the rear bumper—no license plate.

I stood up and quietly stepped over towards my cruiser while keeping one eye on where their light beam landed.

A dozen pairs of eyes snapped up from their grazing near the distant tree line and stared frozen into the bright light.

The fellow with the light turned it off and the noisy car started rolling into the meadow. They were going to try to get closer to the herd before spotting them with a light again and shooting.

I needed to move fast.

I scooted down the slope, opened the driver's door with my right hand and jumped behind the wheel.

I rolled on up behind them while reaching for my radio to alert Tom and Henry.

Then I toggled on my headlights and blues to foul the poachers' plan.

When the crew saw my lights, I heard a yelp in front of me followed by a shout out the window, "Hold on, Billy!"

They were going to make a run for it, despite the threat to life and limb of the fellow perched on the hood.

No problem. Let the games begin.

I punched the accelerator in pursuit and swung way out to the left. If that hood on the hood fell off, I sure didn't want to run over him. I figured I'd come at them from the side.

I hadn't gone but 100 yards when I felt the oil pan slamming on ledge and my car's gas tank bottoming out in muddy dips.

I know if my rig is bottoming out, these fellows are having even more problems. If this was the Jones bunch, their car was one or more bald tires away from the crusher.

At least my vehicle had youth and good springs on its side.

We'd see who made it out of this field with the engine, tranny and axles intact.

I tried the classic "cut 'em off at the pass" western movie maneuver with my spotlight lighting up the field like we were in a movie theater.

And that was appropriate. Because the show I got to see was better than just about any movie.

I know this big farm field. There's a lot of ruts, dips, loops and ledge that make it a challenge even for farm tractors.

Now, we've got deer jackers thinking they are going to outrun my cruiser with a fellow on the hood.

Coming up, I know there's a dip big enough to hide a tank in. If Billy survives this, he should definitely visit Pond Hill some Saturday night and enter.

He makes bull riding look easy. Heck, at least those cowboys have a bull rope. All this kid has for a handhold is a windshield wiper.

I shake my head, slow down and watch it all unfold before my eyes.

Their old car is leaping like a frog with a hungry goose on its behind—the back end of the car is waddling side to side just like the tail of a Canada honker. The bounce in the front of the car makes it clear their ride desperately needs new shock absorbers.

But it was the action on the hood that made my jaw drop. The fellow has his legs spread wide and his backside is bumping up and down a good two feet off the car hood every time the old car slams over ruts and rocks.

I thought I'd seen it all, but this hood rider idea was a new one on me.

My chin about hit the steering wheel and I let up on the gas.

I'm thinking, "This kid is going to get himself killed!"

I'm expecting the driver to back off on the accelerator and give up just to save his human hood ornament from disaster.

But instead, he speeds up. Apparently, he values his freedom more than the life of whoever is on the hood with a hand on the rifle.

Well, I'm not about to let them get away. So, I stomp the accelerator again and keep after them.

The young man on the hood is slamming and rolling like a hot dog on a Hibachi in 30-foot cross current seas—a hot dog with spider legs.

Every time his backside lands on the hood, he tries digging his heels or a toe into some crevice to keep from sliding off over the grill.

I see an arm reach out of the passenger side window trying to grab the bouncing man's shirttail, but there's too much wind.

This is followed by a yelp from the driver, "Dammit Billy! I can't see! Move over, will ya?"

It strikes me there's not a whole lot of compassion within this particular bunch of outlaws.

Their car rocks and rolls over a combination of ledge to the left and deep mud to the right.

It's a whiplash maneuver right out of a monster bucking bull's playbook.

Could this be the maneuver that sends him flying?

The hood rider's backside shoots into the air to

new heights and the look on his face goes from deep concentration to total terror.

The rifle's weight is pulling him off to the right. He's got no choice but to let the gun fly out of his hand. Off it soars into the night.

I make a note to come back and search for it later.

With the rifle gone, he's free to focus on saving his hide. I see his body slam onto the right side of the hood at the bottom of a dip.

He spins onto his side and reaches behind him to slam a hand onto the right wiper blade as a lifeline.

But his trouble isn't over.

When his friends see he's lost the rifle, a howl arises inside the deer jackers' car.

"My gun!" a voice screams out into the night. "Billy's thrown my gun away!"

"I told you we shouldn't oughta brought Billy along!" a deep male voice rages.

More taunts and curses follow as the kid on the hood continues to leap, twirl, slam, crash, stomp and reach for any possible hand or foot hold with his elbows, his knees—even his chin.

I watch as he leaps in the night air like a

salmon fighting the net on Lake Willoughby
and lands with his face plastered against the
windshield.

Maybe he's hoping his baby fuzz chin hair will
grab ahold of the glass?

I know he's been on this steel bull for much
longer than eight seconds. I can't believe he's
doing so well.

I see headlights coming towards me from the
opposite edge of the field and know Tom and
Henry have arrived.

But there's a couple roads leading out of this
big meadow. I'm concerned this driver might
still make it out onto a town road. And if they
do, we could still lose them.

I can't risk real speed on a dirt road with the
possibility of other traffic coming at us and I
can't risk running over this hood hunter.
I'm figuring it's only a matter of time before
he falls.

He's got to be tiring. I see him swinging now
like a broken pendulum, first to the left, then to
the right, slipping and sliding. If his hips slide
too far, onto a fender, he's a goner.

He twists in the air like he's being rolled out of a
blanket and slams his chest onto the windshield
while clawing with his free right hand for the
other wiper.

The car hits another bump and the rider's feet are paddling the air like a cartoon character that's run off a cliff.

His back slams down on the hood and he manages to stomp a sneaker toe against the hood ornament like it's the last piton before a deep crevasse ready to swallow him whole.

I see a tree line ahead and realize the driver is about to intersect the town road.

He's going to have to make a choice of which way to turn—it's a "T."

I'm thinking a 90 degree turn either way will be especially challenging for our big game hunter on the hood.

His biceps have got to be screaming right now and when that old wreck comes roaring out of the farm field, how will he hold on?

Tom and Henry and I speak briefly.

We intend to catch this crew, but not at the expense of this young man's life. We back off to see if they will do the smart thing and stop.

But no dice.

The driver speeds up and dips the old car into the ditch, then spins the steering wheel to the left and punches the gas hard trying to slide out onto the town road.

The twist, dip, buck and goose is too much for
safari man.

With one leap of the car, the rider goes sailing
off the hood end over end like a half filled can
of warm beer tossed into the night.

Looks like we got one.

His buddies leave him there, slide sideways
onto the town road and go roaring off in a cloud
of dust.

I radio Tom and Henry that I'll grab the hood
rider and they should go chasing the vehicle.

I slow to a crawl and aim my light to where
the kid might have landed, get a little closer
and get out and start looking for him with
my flashlight.

I hear some thrashing and moaning off near
the tree line, about 50 feet away from where his
chariot tossed him off and head on over to the
sound.

He's trying to sit up and shaking his head
muttering, "Ow!" and "I can't believe they just
kept going," over and over.

It's Billy Jones.

"Billy, you coulda gotten yourself killed," I say.

"Are you all right? Can you get up?"

"I don't know, Stan. My leg sure don't feel right," he says.

I run my flashlight beam down his jeans and see his foot is not in line with his leg. It's busted all right. The fact he doesn't know it tells me he's going into shock.

"How about we get you to the hospital?" I say. "We can talk on the way."

Billy just nods and says, "Okay." There's no fight in him. He's all done in.

I get him up and hopping on his good leg and load him into the cruiser. I'm just about to throw my rig into drive and head for Gifford Hospital when Tom radios me.

He's found the car about a half mile down the road with its nose buried deep in a basswood tree, the radiator steaming into the night air like a pot of new potatoes and the occupants nowhere to be seen.

Tom tells me he and Henry found fresh blood and deer hair inside the trunk, evidence this crew had taken a deer just a few hours earlier and were intent on a finding another freezer filler when we caught up with them.

On the way to the hospital, Billy and I have a little chat about the evening's activities. He gives me the name of the driver and fellow with the light—a brother and a cousin.

I radio Tom and Henry with the names and they start the search for the other two.

Once at Gifford Hospital, the doctors x-ray Billy's leg, put a cast on it and when they tell me he's good to go some hours later, I load him back into the cruiser.

I head on over to the Woodstock jail and lock him up.

Billy takes it well. It's like a second home to him.

"I hope it's eggs and bacon today for breakfast," he says to the sheriff on duty when we check him in.

With the sun rising in the East, I drive on back to catch up with Tom and Henry. They found Billy's weapon—a small caliber rifle with a dusty scope that had seen better days.

I drive on up to the Jones residence figuring Mrs. Jones might be wondering what had become of her son and to look for more evidence. Deer hair or drops of blood in the driveway might indicate that is where they had stashed the deer they'd taken earlier in the night.

It was about 10 am when I pulled up but in this house, it might as well have been 3 am. The residents had their own unique schedule and for these folks, daylight was time to sleep.

Even the dogs were asleep.

I looked for hair and blood in the driveway, but didn't find any fresh sign. That meant they'd hidden it somewhere else. But as long as I was here, I figured I'd give the family an update. I never knew them to have a phone.

I knocked on the door off and on for several minutes until a sleepy eyed Mrs. Jones answered the door.

"What is it this time, Stan?" she said with a mix of anger and exhaustion, her eyes shutting as soon as she got the question out.

"Billy is in the hospital with a concussion and a broken leg," I said. "I caught him jacking deer last night."

Her eyes open and her brows shoot up a notch. She knows her boys don't generally get hurt hunting from a padded seat inside a car.

Before she can ask, I explain. "Billy was sitting on the hood with a rifle. Danny was driving and he took off in the car trying to get away from me. Billy went flying off the hood into the pucker brush and broke his leg."

There's no gasp or cry of alarm from her about the injury to her boy. This is a lady who has seen about every calamity there is over the years.

"How's the car?" she asks.

"Wrecked," I say. "Danny slammed it into a tree not long after Billy fell off."

Mrs. Jones shuts her eyes. She takes a deep breath, blows out a long slow wheezy whistle between fluttering gray lips, then shakes her head slowly side to side in disgust.

When she opens her eyes a few seconds later, she sighs, and with the resignation of a woman who has survived decades of disappointment, says simply: "Figures."

"Billy's in the Woodstock jail," I add.

She nods, turns, begins to shut the door, then stops. She opens the door wide, turns back to look me in the eye, and speaks to me as one parent to another.

"I sure wish these boys would grow up," she says.

I'd been up all night and now I'm facing hours of writing this colorful incident up for the court. It'll be another three or four hours before I can get some shuteye.

"Me, too," I say. "Me, too."

95

"Our boots are scuffing across snow and gravel
as we slam each other in the ribs, land an elbow
to the face every now and again and roll around
in the middle of the road like there's
some girl at stake."

SNOW BRAWL

CONTRIBUTED BY JOHN KAPUSTA

I came awful close to being the guy inside the pine box on more than one occasion.

I don't know if the attempted knock out punches and occasional shots fired in my direction were due to my charming personality or I just dealt with some unusually tough characters.

I never felt like I had a lot of time to fool with lawbreakers. And I believe if you're afraid, you shouldn't be doing this job.

If fists were thrown, it was because a suspect took the first swing and I was doing my job. Being outnumbered never bothered me— especially when I had Mitzi along with me.

Mitzi was a combination of Rin Tin Tin, Lassie and some sorta mind reading dog all rolled into one. I got her when she was small enough to fit into my cupped palms—a ball of black lab fuzz with curious puppy blue eyes and rubbery little legs.

She grew up to be a really exceptional dog.

She was great with kids in a classroom.
I could have her sit right at a desk with her
paws folded like a student and a dog bone
resting on top of her nose. She wouldn't make
a move to grab and eat it until I told her it was
okay. But out in the field, if she sensed I was
in danger, she turned into a lioness.

Mitzi and I started our years together over
in Rochester but when I was reassigned to
Hardwick, she came with me.

I had a pick up truck at this time and to make
it more comfortable for her, I bought a truck cap
and put together a dog bed in the back for Mitzi.
It wasn't fancy but it was comfortable for her in
all weather.

The cap had a panel over the tailgate with
piston pump arms at either side to make it easy
to lift up. If she was in the truck bed, I'd leave
the latch unlocked when I stepped out of the
cab, so if Mitzi wanted to get out, she could.
I knew she wouldn't take off on me.

More than once I'd pull the truck over and
be talking with a few fishermen or hunters,
asking to see their licenses, and maybe one
or two of them would start to raise their
voices a little.

If Mitzi were riding with me that day, she'd hear
them and be at my side in a flash.

If her sudden appearance didn't prompt a fellow

to show a little more respect for the badge,
she had another tool in her canine kit.

She would stare right at the fellow's throat,
the hair on her back would start to rise up and
she'd launch into a low growl.

That generally gave any fellow who wanted to
argue the finer points of fish and game law
enforcement with me an immediate attitude
adjustment.

Mitzi wasn't the biggest lab in the world by
any means, but she just had this presence that
made it very clear she was all business if she
felt I was in any danger.

I raised and trained a lot of dogs and felt she
was pretty exceptional.

But on a cold November night in Stannard,
she proved it.

It was early November around 9 pm and some
snow had fallen on top of what had already
been kinda greasy roads earlier in the day.

Rifle season was underway and it was the
busiest time of year for wardens. I was on patrol
riding the back roads of Greensboro and on over
to Stannard.

I could feel and hear the snow and slush
beneath my truck tires turning to ice as the
temperatures dipped way below freezing.

I round a bend and see a car pointed towards me pulled way over to the right with its headlights on bright and clouds of exhaust steaming out of the rear pipe. There looks to be one or two guys pushing hard on the trunk.

I knew immediately that the driver had gone too far to the right and dropped the right front wheel into the ditch.

I drive on by until I can find a place to seesaw my truck around. I'm wanting to help get them unstuck.

As I drive back up the road and come up on the vehicle from behind, I see one guy with his shoulder on the trunk pushing hard and the other lifting up the rear bumper.

The driver is about flooring the accelerator, because his rear wheel is spinning fast enough to burn rubber on snow and dig down into the gravel beneath.

I'm 60 feet away and rolling up on them when the car finally gets traction and leaps forward out of the ditch. The guys at the back chase after the driver and pile inside like they are running from a bank robbery.

The car roars off down the road, fish tailing madly.

Well, that's pretty odd behavior out here in the middle of the night.

Downright suspicious.

What was going to be a good deed on my part is now looking like I need to introduce myself and have a little chat.

So, I flip on my blue lights and follow them.

The driver speeds up.

I punch my truck's accelerator and add the siren.

They go faster.

I try to make out their car's license plate, but with snow flying up, I can't see much except that it's not from Vermont. It looks to have a white or yellow background.

I follow them for miles. Way up near Flagg Pond on Gonyaw Road, the driver loses control, their car climbs a bank of trees and finally tips over onto its side.

When I roll up on the scene, the wheels are still spinning and the headlights are still on. I park about 30 feet away and train my spotlight on the vehicle.

You don't rush up on a scene like this for a number of reasons—the least of which is the vehicle can catch fire. Another is, the people in the car might have some firepower of their own.

I reach for my radio to call in the accident.
As I talk to the Dispatcher, three young fellows
clamber out of the car and scatter like partridge
chicks into the woods.

I cock my head and read the rear license plate
on the overturned car. It's from New Mexico.

I didn't know what was up, but I had a funny
feeling that maybe there was something bigger
going on here than just an out of Towner
wanting to take a cheap shot at a whitetail.

I let the Dispatcher know my location near
Flagg Pond with an overturned vehicle and three
suspects headed for a very cold night in the
woods.

If there's an officer available, I could use some
help rounding them up, I admit.

That's when I see a plume of steam coming
from the front of the overturned car.

Looks like the radiator is leaking or a hose has
blown. "We'll be needing a tow truck, too," I
advise.

The Dispatcher tells me she will send some
backup as soon as it's available.

Well, it wasn't my style to sit tight in the truck
and just wait for reinforcements.

I locked the truck cab—I always kept an extra

set of keys in my wallet—and I walked to the
back of my truck, opened the truck cap and
called to Mitzi.

With my blue lights on and the truck idling but
locked, I went on foot patrol looking to catch at
least one of these fellows.

I didn't get a good look at any of them, but they
didn't appear to be dressed for a cold night in
the woods. None of them were wearing gloves
or mittens.

A few minutes stumbling about in a foot of
snow in these below zero temperatures should
make them change their minds about running
off.

Whatever made them run, freezing to death
had to be a worse choice than facing me, I was
guessing.

I walked down the road, looking for their tracks.

I rounded a bend maybe 100 yards from the
accident, shining my light back and forth
across the roadway, when the shadow of a man
appeared about 50 feet in front of me.

I turned my light on him as he approached.
He had on a tight T shirt under a black leather
vest, jeans, cowboy boots and a thick brimmed
leather hat.

He was walking towards me with a confident

swagger, palms open and facing me to indicate he was no threat.

He looked to be the fellow that had jumped out of the driver's side when the car landed on its side.

"Stop right there! You're under arrest," I said, as he got within 20 feet of me.

"Easy there, Sheriff!" he said. "What are you talking about? I ain't done nothin'," and he kept coming at me with a big grin on his face like he was a long lost friend about to buy me a beer.

"I'm not a sheriff. I'm a game warden. You took off when I turned on my lights and siren. That's evading an officer. You're under arrest," I said. "Now, turn around and give me your hands."

"Ah come on, now," he said with a bit of a drawl, "I'm sure we can work this out," and he kept walking right on up to me.

He got to within 10 feet of me and that's when I saw he had a good 40 pounds on me—muscle, not fat—and more than a foot in height.

He saw it, too. He grinned bigger.

"We were just doin' a little joy riding is all. Ain't no harm done. We'll just get the car back on its wheels and be on our way," he says.

"Not until I get some answers," I say.

"Now, turn around and give me your hands."

He drew a big breath, looked down at me from a couple feet away, stopped in his tracks and scowled.

"Turn around," I said again.

That's when he dropped the big Western howdy smile.

"No way," the giant said and he lunged and swung a huge roundhouse punch at my jaw, intended to knock me down and out.

I stood my ground, tucked my chin to my chest and felt the breeze. His big fist missed my chin by less than an inch.

He spun on his boot heel and started running back down the road.

I chased after him.

He was in good shape, but his smooth bottomed cowboy boots were no match for ice and snow.

His feet were slipping and sliding like a cheap toupee on a bald man at poolside on a 102 degree day.

I had the advantage with the rubber lug soles on my boots.

I ran up behind him and threw myself on his

back like the football coach had taught us back at Burr and Burton Academy. I managed to knock the cowboy face down into the snow and ice all right, but that was just the beginning.

He wasn't about to give up.

He started squirming and thrashing like a snake that's had his tail stepped on—a big snake.

This guy had forearms like a longshoreman and legs like a linebacker.

I'm rugged, but he's huge.

We're in the middle of the snow and gravel road throwing punches at each other, gouging chins, exchanging kicked shins and stomped ankles.

It doesn't take me long to figure out that this guy is serious about maybe killing me. I don't know what he's hiding or what he's got going on, but he's fighting like a man who has a lot to lose.

"Give up," I say, and he just grunts and snarls and tries to head butt me.

The two of us are groaning and punching and wrestling for control for a good 10 minutes.

I've got his T shirt about torn off his back. He's ripped out the shoulder of my jacket.

Our boots are scuffing across snow and gravel as we slam each other in the ribs, land an elbow to the face every now and again and roll around in the middle of the road like there's some girl at stake.

I never heard the second guy come up behind us.

All of a sudden I feel a powerful yank at my right hip—so hard it snaps my head and neck back—and I realize someone has gone for my sidearm.

I hear the heavy thread of my holster ripping and the weight of my revolver being lifted up and ripped right off my belt.

There's nothing I can do. I can't so much as turn my head and look up because I'm in the fight of my life with this bruiser.

He's pounding on me and trying to land a knock out punch.

A knife of ice cold terror races through me as I realize my .357 is in the hands of some guy standing behind me.

I'm thinking, "Oh my God. This is it." But I push that feeling away and try to focus on getting the upper hand in this fight.

I shift my hips, to try and flip the bigger man on top of me. I want to block any shot the fellow

107

holding my gun might have, to make it harder
for him to pull the trigger.

I figure he won't want to take a chance on
shooting his buddy.

But the big man I'm fighting is tough to turn.
It's clear he's an experienced wrestler.

I keep punching and weaving my head,
hoping to find an opening that will allow me
to escape the shot that I'm certain will come
any second.

I'm sweating and straining and freezing and
punching and praying for a miracle.

The big man beneath me grins like Lucifer.

I figure he's seen his buddy behind me aiming
my .357 at the back of my head.

Three seconds later, I hear a scream behind
me—a mix of rage and pain.

It echoes off the hills and stops both me and the
cowboy in mid punch.

What the...?

I turn my head and see a man spinning like
a top in the road, twisting and screaming
in agony, swinging his arms behind him.
corkscrewing himself into the snow bank and
then stumbling back down into the road.

There's something on his back. It's Mitzi and
she's buried her teeth into the muscles of his
right shoulder and forced him to drop my gun.

And she ain't letting go.

The guy is wailing, begging for help, crying
and screaming. He can't spin fast enough to
shake her loose. When he grabs her hind leg,
she sinks her teeth in deeper and shakes the
muscle in his back.

Say what you want about Labradors being
all love and no teeth, this night Mitzi turned in
her AKC lab papers and decided she was
a bulldog.

For all this fellow knew it was a wolf or
Sasquatch that sunk her fangs into him.

Mitzi wasn't one for barking. She just got the
job done.

With his buddy stumbling about, screaming
and pleading for help, the bruiser who's been
bashing me softens his punches a little.

I suspect he figures whatever is tearing his
friend's back apart is going to be chewing on
him next if he doesn't give up.

"The dog will be on you next! Give up!" I snarl.

And this time, Hercules says, "All right!
All right!" and lets me go.

A couple seconds later I hear a "thump" and I
see the fellow with Mitzi on his back crumble
into a heap.

It was the police chief from over in Hardwick.
He'd knocked the fellow out with his flashlight.

When Mitzi feels the assailant go limp, she
jumps off his back and comes running over to
the man in the black leather vest.

Mitzi—glaring at him—changes his attitude fast.

"Hey, keep that dog off of me, okay?" he said.
"I'm done. I'm done. Just keep the dog away."

The chief and I handcuff and load these two
fellows into his cruiser where they are taken
to jail.

I stay behind to wait for the tow truck and
continue to look for the third suspect.

We learned the car was stolen in New Mexico.
I came back at first light and searched again
for the third fellow, but I never caught up
with him.

My sense was he was a local boy who knew
how to get out of the area. I think he'd gotten
in over his head when he decided to join
these two.

The pair of outlaws were arraigned before
a judge on charges of attempting to elude,

resisting arrest, operating a vehicle without the owner's consent and assault on a law officer.

I was back out in the woods the next morning—a little sore and black and blue, but the uniform covered most of it up.

It was the busiest time of year for me—deer rifle season—and I didn't feel comfortable taking the day off to sit in court for hours waiting for this pair to be arraigned.

I trusted the State's Attorney to do his job and put these two behind bars.

In retrospect, I guess I shoulda been at the courthouse.

I don't know whether the State's Attorney didn't have time to read the report I'd written or he didn't think it was that serious or the judge was the problem or what all happened.

All I know is the judge let these two fellows—with no ties to Vermont—go on personal recognizance. He cited them to appear at a later date.

They must have thought they'd won the attempted murderer lottery.

They disappeared before the ink was dry and were never seen or heard from again.

But while the courts might not have taken what happened to me that night seriously, word spread quickly through the warden and police grapevine.

A few days later I'm getting calls asking me if I want to sell my dog.

Hmmmmmm. How much did I think my life was worth?

I said I'd pass.

But I did decide she might like to put her mama bear instincts to good use and have some pups of her own to guard.

So, I introduced her to a handsome black lab with a suitable pedigree and good manners and they hit it off.

Before long, I had the pitter patter of puppy paws all over the house and a line of guys who wanted one of Mitzi's pups.

I set aside a female from the litter for my deputy warden and friend, Art Chase.

Art and I shared quite a few adventures over the years and I wanted to thank him.

Art and his wife agreed it would be nice for his kids to have a dog to play with, as well as a guardian.

According to Art, Mitzi's daughter grew into a good companion—a lot like her mama—but not exactly.

"She was a good dog," Art explains, "but every once in awhile she'd do this kinda strange thing."

"I'd be wrestling with the kids or the wife—you know, just playin' around in the yard—and that dog would sneak up on me, jump up and bite me right in the behind!

"Tore my pants a couple times and it hurt, too!"

"I held the bag up about two inches from the fellow's nose, shined the light into his eyes and asked, "Is this yours?"

KNIFEMAN

CONTRIBUTED BY BOB LUTZ

I t was early September when I got the call from a couple over near French Hill Road in Fairfield.

The caller was a woman, who said she and her husband had heard a gunshot the night before that had raised them from their beds.

Looking out the window, the woman said her husband had seen red taillights of what he believed to be a pickup truck. The vehicle had sat there idling for a bit then drove away fast.

They believed someone had poached a deer. Trouble was, they had waited until morning to call and tell me. Wardens like to be called immediately, regardless of the time.

I didn't have a lot of hope of finding much evidence since so much time had passed, but I drove on over to talk to them.

A pair of friendly, well fed Golden Retrievers ran out to greet me when I pulled in.

They were a retired couple with a newly built

home sitting on a hill. They were pretty solid on the time they heard a shot and the approximate location, but short on details.

They had not seen anyone shoot. They didn't get a license plate number. They had no idea if this was just one person acting alone or two.

All the fellow could really tell me is he had seen the taillights of what he believed to be a pickup truck. He pointed out the approximate location as we talked on their front porch.

"I'm sorry we can't tell you more," the wife said. "I hope we didn't call you here for nothing."

I told them not to be shy about calling me late at night if this happened again. I explained I worked all hours of the day and night and would come right out.

Then I promised to go take a look and report back to them what I found.

I walked down the dirt road in the general direction they had given me. It didn't take me long to find a trampled section of grass at the edge of the dirt road and blood evidence.

There were even some lugged tire tracks in the tall grass next to the traveled portion of the road. That indicated the poacher's truck was sporting winter tires.

I followed the trail into the field. The poacher had field dressed his kill in the dark to lighten his load hauling it out of this field before he drove off.

I looked about for boot prints and other evidence to help me build a case.

Guys have been known to drop their wallets, a business card and even house keys in their hurry to get away. You never know what you might find. It pays to look hard.

The sun was rising and a beam glinted off something shiny lying on top of the pile.

It was a knife. Not a hunting knife with a big blade, but a utility knife, the kind used to cut sheetrock and vinyl flooring.

Did this guy use a utility knife to field dress his deer?

I pick up the tool, and wipe the blood on some tall grass, retract the blade and take a closer look at the handle. Maybe it has a mark on it that could help me identify the owner.

That's when I saw the name.

LUTZ.

In big letters on the handle was my last name.

What? I felt the blood rise in my cheeks.

This poacher left this knife here on purpose, just to taunt me?

My mind started racing into big time anger. If this guy wanted to humiliate me, by inference he wanted to insult all wardens everywhere.

"Okay, buddy, if that's the game you wanna play, I'm in," I muttered to myself.

Suddenly a routine case was anything but.

It was clear to me this guy had left that knife as a challenge.

I reached for an evidence bag inside my coat and dropped the knife inside.

I am going to catch this guy if it's the last thing I do.

I studied the scene and took as many notes as I could. But other than the knife and part of a boot print, there really wasn't much.

I walked back up to the residence and talked again to the witnesses. I didn't tell them about the knife. I just told them they were right—someone had taken a deer last night.

I asked them again if there was anything else they could recall about the truck that might help me identify it or the driver.

That's when the husband told me he believed he'd seen a ladder rack above the truck bed and that maybe the tailgate was two-toned as well.

"Any idea as to the color of the truck?" I ask him.

"Sorry, it was just too dark," he said.

Well, it wasn't much but it was something.

I urged them to call me if they thought of anything else and left.

For the next few days, I haunted the local lumberyards, hoping to spot a pick up truck that matched the description the couple had given me. And I ran a list of all the cases I'd had the last couple of years that might prompt a guy to react this way.

I guessed that the suspect was a drywall contractor, that he was local and would routinely be stopping into hardware stores and lumberyards for sheetrock, drywall tape, mud and other supplies.

So, I visited a lot of parking lots, strolling by trucks while the owners were in the stores. I was hoping to spot deer hair or blood in the truck bed, stuck to a fender or bumper.

Sometimes looking into the cab through a passenger window helps, too. Maybe there would be shells on the seat or evidence of blood or a jacket with some blood on it—something.

Once I found the truck, I could run the license plate number and identify the owner.

In the days and weeks that followed, I looked at hundreds of pickups and ran record checks on a dozen or so that remotely fit the description the home owner had given me.

Guys have been known to try and disguise their truck after they've taken deer. So, it wasn't out of the realm of possibility the owner had taken the rack off, but I figured this guy didn't suspect anyone had seen him.

I saw maybe a couple hundred pickups—but not one truck that had a ladder rack and a two toned tailgate and snow tires.

And even when I strolled through parking lots looking at trucks that might remotely fit even part of the description, there wasn't a shred of evidence of hair or blood anywhere on them.

I tried another tactic. I made calls to friends in the building trades—asking if they knew anyone boasting about taking a deer out of season or if they had heard of anyone selling venison or if they knew of any laborer driving a truck like the one I was looking for.

Nothing.

The trail was stone cold.

Weeks passed.

New cases came up. I was plenty busy. This case sifted to the bottom of the pile.

But lying awake at night and going over my "to do" list for the next day, finding the guy who left that knife would come back and haunt me.

It sorta hung over my head like a dark cloud.

Rifle season came. I kept an eye open at the deer check in stations, figuring this guy might pull in to weigh his buck using that same truck. Nothing.

When December's muzzleloader season came and went without a suspect, I knew this case was never going to be solved unless the guy screwed up big time.

Still, it bothered me. And I kept my eyes and ears open for clues and maybe the chance he would try it again.

It was late February, almost six months after I'd found the knife, when I got a late night call from Dispatch asking me to assist on a car accident involving a deer, not far from where the deer jacking had taken place.

I rolled out of bed, dressed quickly and headed out into the frosty night. I found the car pretty well banged up. The driver was fine, but the deer didn't make it.

I was just finishing up getting a statement from the driver and directing traffic around the scene, when I heard a loud vehicle approach from behind me.

Whatever it was had a serious hole in its exhaust not too far back from the manifold. Not too many Harleys on snow packed roads.

The roar prompted me to look up. The headlights were shining in my eyes, making it hard to see clearly.

I looked beneath the lights to see a truck coming at me with a twisted front bumper and big lug tires. This was definitely a work vehicle that had seen better days. As it rolled up beside me, I saw it was faded red with some shade of tan or beige on the side panels.

The driver slowed way down in an attempt to roll past without touching the gas pedal—trying to keep a low profile—but he rubbernecked to check out the accident scene as he went by.

My eyes stayed on the flopping front and rear fenders as the truck slid past me in the snow choked lane.

It was as if I was trying to remember something but wasn't quite sure what it was—like when you awake in the morning from a dream and you want to hold onto the elements to try and make some sense of it.

When the driver saw me looking at his truck, he snapped his head back to the left to look straight ahead at the road.

Hunh. That's odd. Innocent folks don't do that.

The truck rolls on past me putt putting like an old Harley rolling to a stop. I'm still unable to tear myself away from staring at it, but I don't

know why. It's got working taillights and a
current green and white license plate, despite
being a winter beater rig.

I look higher and see a faded red and some sorta
ugly brownish tailgate.

I stand there staring at the truck as it rolls away
into the night. What is it about this truck?

I look up from the tailgate and see a steel ladder
rack—a homemade one. Practical, not fancy.

I start adding it up: beater truck, snow tires,
ladder rack, two color tailgate.

My brain fog lifts.

Is this the poacher from last September who left
the knife there to insult me?

I grabbed my pen and scribbled down the license
plate number.

Then I ran to my cruiser and threw it into
first gear low and just rolled along behind the
suspect's truck, keeping him in my sights but
not sitting on his bumper.

I called into Dispatch and asked them to run the
registration. The plate came back registered to a
guy I had never heard of before.

In an area with this few people, that was
unusual.

And it was likely also part of the reason he hadn't been on my short list of guys with an attitude who just might think leaving a knife there with my name on the handle was funny.

I followed the truck up and down hills for a mile or so.

We weren't far from an intersection where we would encounter heavier traffic. I decided to pull him over while the traffic was minimal.

The truck's defective exhaust gave me probable cause to stop the driver. It was not something I would routinely do, but I had the legal authority to do it.

I just had to find out if this was the poacher I'd had been hunting for months.

I turned on my blue lights and the driver immediately pulled over into the snow bank along the road. He knew I'd been following him.

Before walking up to the truck cab, I reached back into my tool kit behind me and reached for the evidence bag.

My hand landed right on it—like a key piece of a jigsaw puzzle that leaps out at you even though your eyes are closed.

I held the bag up under the dome light just to make certain. The deer blood on the knife was now black, but the name "Lutz" was still clearly

visible on the handle through the clear plastic.
With my flashlight in my left hand and the
evidence bag in my right, I walked cautiously
but confidently up to the pickup truck driver.

He shut off the truck, rolled his window down
and waited for me.

I am not one for small talk when something has
been eating at me. I cut right to the chase.

I held the bag up about two inches from the
fellow's nose, shined the light into his eyes and
asked, "Is this yours?"

Sometimes you get lucky.

There was a two second pause followed by,
"Yeah, it's mine."

It was that easy.

"Well, leave the parking lights on and get out of
the cab slowly with your hands up," I told him.

He was clean—no weapons on him.

"Come on back into my cruiser and let's talk,"
I said.

That was a mistake.

This fellow wouldn't shut up.

The story he told went like this: He had come on

up to the area from Connecticut to be with a girl and then cabin fever set in the winter before and they broke up. He signed on with a carpenter as an extra pair of hands, and had been working his way up into sheetrock hanging and painting.

He'd made friends with some of the locals and they invited him to go deer hunting last summer.

He'd bought a rifle in preparation for the upcoming deer season and was just coming back from sighting in his new rifle with his pals after a couple beers to celebrate last September, when this nice buck ran in front of him.

"It was like the deer gods were talking to me," he said. "Of course, I'd had a few beers."

Rifle season was weeks away, but he couldn't wait. A shiny new rifle, fresh box of shells, no one around, and fresh venison for the taking was within his reach.

He slammed the brakes, glanced ahead and behind the truck, saw no one was around, rammed three shells quickly into the rifle, rolled down the passenger side window, shined a flashlight into the field and saw the deer just staring back at him.

He rested an elbow on the armrest of the passenger door, took a deep breath and squeezed the trigger. "He went down with one shot," he said.

A lot of guys, even in a confession, just can't resist the urge to brag about their kill—as if shooting a deer standing in the open, blinded by a light, while leaning on a truck door takes a lot of skill.

Trust me, it doesn't.

Right after he got the buck home, the guilt started to set in, he said, along with the fear of being discovered.

He took his truck off the road and hid it, just in case anyone had seen it. He told his friends the head gasket had blown.

"I've been looking over my shoulder for months. I've had a lot of sleepless nights," he said. "It feels good to just admit this and get it over with."

I explained that I would write him a citation for taking a deer out of season, and if he would like to plead guilty he could avoid a court appearance. He'd lose his license for three years and pay a hefty fine.

I let him know I could ask a judge to take his truck and rifle, too. But since it was his first offense—and I hoped his last—I would go easy on him.

He thanked me for that.

But the knife was still eating at me. In all of his long confession, he'd never once mentioned the knife or why he had left it behind and why he wanted to taunt me with it.

I couldn't let him leave the cruiser without an explanation. I had to ask.

"So, uh, what was up with the knife?"

"What?" he said.

"Why did you leave that knife behind?" I asked him, pointing to the evidence bag on the dash in front of us.

"My hands were shaking something fierce and the handle just got really slippery. The knife slid right out of my hand and I just lost sight of it. I didn't dare turn on my flashlight. I saw a light go on in a house across the road. That scared me even more. I just grabbed the deer and took off and left it behind."

"What about the name on the knife?" I asked him.

"What?" he said. He cocked his head off to the right a bit. In the light of the cab with a crown of curly blond hair on his head, he looked a lot like a cocker spaniel puppy.

"The name on the handle," I reminded him.

He looked at me totally confused. "Come again?" he said trying to be polite.

"L-U-T-Z," I said, leaning into him and pointing to the name tag above my breast pocket on my uniform. "Lutz is my last name. And that's the name on the knife handle."

"Really?" he said in amazement. And he leaned in closer under the dome light to read my name tag, and then squinted at the knife in the baggie.

"Hunh! Well, don't that beat all," he said, and chuckled at the coincidence.

"You know, I actually got that knife for free. The hardware store was giving them away a year or so ago," he said. "It was a promotion for something or other. I don't really remember what."

He looked me right in the eye as innocent as a teenager who didn't know the cupcakes on the counter were for Mom's fancy dinner party and he'd already eaten a half dozen of them.

"I never even noticed there was a name on the handle."

"Oh," I said.

And right then, I kinda went drifty for a minute.

My mind was recollecting all the hours I'd spent staking out lumberyards and hardware stores looking for this guy, for his truck, for revenge.

I'd created this whole big story about this case—of a clever guy with a grudge and a vendetta. I'd turned him into Moby Dick and Moriarity both. I'd gotten my shorts in a big bunch for months—over a bumbling poacher's dropped knife.

I thought of all the sleepless hours, all the anger I'd felt—enough to spike my blood pressure through the roof.

Now, I've caught him, and he's nothing more than another guy with an itchy trigger finger that let a couple beers and buck fever get the best of him.

There's no big vendetta against me or my fellow wardens. He didn't even know my name. Hunh.

The silence bothers him.

He turns towards me and says, "Uh, geez, Warden, this knife seems to mean an awful lot to you. How about you just keep it? I got others."

I snap back into full consciousness and look at him. Is he trying to bribe me? The look on his face says otherwise. He's just trying to be nice.

"Thanks, but that knife is evidence," I tell him. "You'll get it back when your case is resolved."

I turn him loose with a citation. He thanks me and apologizes again for breaking the law, before he climbs in his truck and drives off.

Nice guy.

I throw the cruiser into Drive and head home.
But something doesn't feel right. I'd solved
the case. But I wasn't so sure I'd solved the
problem.

The next day, I swing into the lumberyard and
buy myself a Lutz utility knife, just like the one
he'd used. I toss it onto the dash of my truck,
where I can see it every day.

That knife rode shotgun with me for many miles,
right up until the day I retired.

Like the young fellow said, it came in handy for
a lot of jobs: cutting a hank of rope, slicing open
boxes, peeling insulation off wiring, trimming
sheetrock and vinyl flooring.

But the job that Lutz knife did best was
reminding me not to take things so personally.

Sometimes, a knife is just a knife.

"It's a risky move, because once we get
ahold of her tail, what then?
Do you declare victory just before
you're clawed to pieces?"

COUGAR

CONTRIBUTED BY JOHN KAPUSTA

Catamount. Cougar. Puma. Panther. Mountain Lion. Ghost Cat. Seems like every culture settling the Americas created a unique name for our biggest native wildcat. There's dozens of labels for the animal that is at home in the Yukon to the Andes.

Whatever you want to call them, I believe I'm the only warden in the last century who can honestly say I wrestled a live panther here in the Green Mountains.

I got a call saying a child had been attacked by a cougar at Stub Earle's shop on Lake Eden.

Ernest, "Stub" Earle was a member of the Vermont House of Representatives at the time, and he just happened to serve on the Fish & Wildlife Committee.

Stub's Stop Over was a bait shop, grocery store, a place to make a phone call, get directions, buy gas and purchase a fishing license. There was an adjoining campground and you could walk down to the lake and rent a rowboat.

It had about all you needed and was a busy hub for locals and visitors.

But a cougar attack at Stub's Stop Over?

Someone had to be pulling my leg.

I didn't believe it, but I responded as if I did. You have to.

I ran out of my house in Hardwick, checked to make certain my large animal cage was in the back of my truck, jumped behind the wheel and headed out towards Eden wondering what I'd find.

Probably it was just a neighbor's big house cat that had jumped up on a picnic table and taken a swipe at a camper's tuna sandwich.

Or maybe it could be a hungry bobcat that had wandered over to Stub's after it got scent of fish someone had caught and cleaned at the dock. If so, it would have to be a sick bobcat, because they prefer to hunt in the shadows like their bigger cousins.

No way did I believe I would come face to face with a live catamount.

It was about as good a tall tale as a Big Foot sighting.

When I pulled into the Stop Over parking lot, a fellow ran out from under the shade of a big cottonwood tree towards my truck.

He was wringing his hands and his eyes were wide. It was clear this was a man dying to share information. I rolled down my window to listen to his story.

It's a good one. Here's what he said:

"I was planning on a nice afternoon of fishing for perch and sight seeing here on the lake. I'd rented a rowboat and was down at the shore getting ready to push off when up above me I heard a high pitched squeal.

I looked up and saw a girl, maybe six or seven years old. She was dressed in a bathing suit and had a life vest on and she was shouting to her mother to hurry—waving her arms and jumping up and down—all excited and laughing in that squealy screamy annoying voice little girls use when they're all excited and eager to get going.

Once I saw she was okay, I picked up my oars and pushed off from shore with my tackle box, cooler and pole beside me.

I turned my head to make sure no boat was behind me coming into the dock. I started to row out and was maybe 10 feet from shore when I heard a scream—a god awful ear piercing scream.

I looked up and I saw the little girl bent over

and there's this big cat biting her neck—or trying to anyway. The cat was standing on its hind legs and had one paw on her shoulder and the other part way around her waist. It was sinking its teeth into the life preserver she was wearing.

I yelled and jumped out of the rowboat into the water and grabbed the only thing I could think of to battle the cat—an oar.

I yanked the oar out of the lock and ran shouting and swinging the paddle onto shore and up the steps.

The cat is smart. It was pushing on the girl, taking a step forward on its hind feet, to get the kid to fall to her knees. The girl is whimpering now and crying and her eyes are shut tight. I don't know if she ever even saw what had grabbed ahold of her.

Anyhow, I got up to within six feet of the cat and I just start wacking on it with the oar.

I couldn't swing for the cougar's head because I might hit the girl. But I smacked that cat in the ribs and I tried knocking its hind legs out from under it.

But it just bit down harder on her collar, like a barn cat that doesn't want to share the mouse it just caught.

And it turned its head a little to look at me, like

it was saying, 'Brother, this is my kill and you'd better leave me alone!' Let me tell you, that was a look I'll never forget!

I knew I had to try harder so I took a big step back and swung that oar like I was in Fenway and hit the cat as hard as I could. I caught her right in the head.

That did it. Finally, she let go and jumped off. She kinda hunkered down low and went slinking off under the deck next to the steps.

The guy pauses and stands there shaking his head like he can't even believe his own story.

"What about the girl?" I asked him.

"As soon as the cat was gone, I grabbed her with one arm and dragged her away, out into the yard. A few seconds later, her mother showed up."

"Where's the girl now?" I asked.

"Her mother took her to the hospital to be checked out. That orange life vest—it saved her life. The cougar got a mouth full of stuffing and nothing else, I don't think. She might be scratched up a little. But I think she's was mostly just scared."

"Where's the life preserver?"

"The girl's mother just scooped up her daughter

and ran to the car and put her inside and took off once I told her what happened. She was still wearing it as they drove off," he tells me.

I'm listening to his story and still wondering if this guy is pulling my leg. There's no victim here for me to examine, no blood, not even the life preserver—just a big story.

Even if some animal did attack a child, I can't believe a cougar was the culprit. Maybe a bobcat or some feral cat?

"You say this was a cougar?"

"Yeah, I know it's a cougar."

"How do you know?" I asked him.

"Tan, tall as me," he says, "with a real long tail."

He sees me looking at him kinda skeptical and adds, "Look, I'm no big game hunter, but I know the difference between a bobcat and a cougar, Warden. This ain't a bobcat. This is the real deal—a cougar or catamount or whatever you want to call it."

I don't smell alcohol on his breath. His eyes are clear. Still, this story is one of the wildest I've been told in all my years on the job. I'm wondering if maybe he's delusional.

"Oh! One more thing. This cat is wearing a collar and towing a chain."

138

Well, that set me back on my heels. Why would he make that part up?

"A collar and a chain, you say?"

"Yeah. Maybe it escaped from a circus or a zoo or something?"

"Did you get hurt?" I ask. "Any scratches or bites or ?" taking a closer look at the fellow as I open the truck door and grab my gear.

"No. The cat never touched me."

"Show me where you last saw it," I said.
"But let me go first—you stay behind me,"
I cautioned.

He nodded and said, "Okay, head out towards the lake."

I was familiar with Stub's set up. He used the space under the back porch as storage for all manner of supplies.

There were canoes and paddles and Sunfish sailboats and sails, oars and lumber piled up, tent poles—you name it, he could probably find it under there somewhere.

That meant this storage area was a maze of dark corners and varying elevations—perfect for a cat to crouch and hide in.

If this cat really was wearing a collar, it was

used to humans. But that didn't mean it was tame.

Still, if the cat had calmed down from it's attack mode, I might be able to catch it without having to kill it. It might be licking its wounds as a result of being clobbered by the fellow with the oar.

Then again, it might be in a lot of pain and be ready to fight for its life.

One thing was for sure—I wasn't going to be able to have a conversation with the animal and talk it into coming with me peaceably.

I flicked the keeper on my holster up, so I could save a split second if I needed to reach for my revolver as I headed towards the staircase leading to the lake.

"How far down was the girl? How many steps?" I ask the fellow as I get close to the deck.

"Maybe five or six steps or so? I'm not sure," he says.

"All right. Well, how about you help me out by going back out to the parking lot and making certain no one comes over this way. I don't want anybody else hurt."

"Got it," he says and smiles. He's a fellow who likes to have a job to do.

And now, I have one less person to worry about.

Now, it's just me and who knows what? I'm about to find out.

I'm looking for a tail tip flick, eye shine, or maybe the sound of a chain rattle as I step from bright summer sun into the cool dark of the deck's interior and freeze. I stop to let my eyes adjust to the shadows.

My flashlight is back in the truck. I don't want to take the time to go get it and risk this animal taking off into the neighborhood of summer camps and motor homes.

There's a lot of people outdoors enjoying the day and the cat might well attack again or be provoked into defending itself.

As far as I know, this little corner of the world doesn't know there's a panther on the loose and that's fine with me. I'm hoping the cougar—if that's what this really is—won't be loose long.

If I was a cougar, where would I want to hide? Well, cats like to be up high. So, I am thinking if there is any stack of lumber or a keel up sailboat hanging by some ropes with a little room to spare, that's where the big cat will be crouched. Or maybe in a corner? Then again, some cats like to crawl into a corner and hide.

I take another step, stop and listen and realize, the animal could be anywhere in here. Cats see in the dark and can hear a mouse 100 feet away.

If there is a cougar under here, it has all the advantages in this hide and seek, life or death game. It knows exactly where I am.

I take another step into the dark, listening intently for any movement in the shadows, peering into the corners, when I hear a man shouting maybe 20 feet behind me, outside the deck.

He's a combination of angry and defensive. There's another man speaking and a shouting match starting up.

I turned and saw a fellow in a muscle man shirt, jeans and biker boots poking his head under the deck. He's calling, "Carla! Carla! Come here, girl!" like he's lost his dog or maybe—just maybe—a cougar.

"Get out of here before you get hurt," I said.

"I'm after my cat," he said.

"You mean your cougar?" I challenge him.

"Well, uh...." He tripped over his words and his own boots. He's seen my badge and doesn't want to admit he knows what I'm talking about.

"Can you get it to come out of here?" I asked him.

"Yeah, sure," he said. "Carla's just a big pussycat."

I decided not to argue with the guy about how sweet his pet is at this moment.

The fellow heads over to a center post behind a stack of boxes and I heard the rattling of a chain being lifted and dragged across stones and earth.

"Ah! There you are! Come on, girl. Good kitty!" he says in a cuddly cute voice to an animal I still can't see.

But there's the sound of something solid dropping to the ground—a kind of padded whoosh—maybe 15 feet in front of me and a little to my right, followed by the clatter of the chain being gathered up.

"Good girl," the fellow says again, followed by, "Maybe you should back up outta here. It's kind of tight and I'm coming out with her."

I step back out into the sunlight, but I don't turn around. I'm eager to see just what he has on the end of that chain.

I'm five paces back out into the sunlight when a long tawny colored cat with close ears, yellow eyes and paws bigger than my hands comes strolling out from under the deck followed closely by a tattooed 30 year old fellow holding her back with a dog run chain.

No doubt about it—I'm looking at a mountain lion, and she's a beauty.

The animal appears to weigh about 110 pounds. Her tail is at least half as long as she is with a touch of black at the tip.

Her eyes are taking in every little bird flitting in the trees, the slightest sound—she doesn't miss a trick—even though her focus is straight ahead.

It's time to get some answers.

"This cat belong to you?" I ask the fellow holding the chain.

"Well, uh….to the club…" He tries to dance around as to who owns the cat and how it got here and the details.

But after some more discussion, he tells me he's part of a motorcycle club from somewhere outside of New York City and this panther is their mascot. They bought it as a kitten a year or more ago. The club decided to come to Vermont for some rest and recreation and they thought it would be nice to bring the cougar, whose name is Carla, with them. Says they named it after the feisty waitress in the TV show, Cheers.

I don't say anything, but as I recall from watching that show, Carla the waitress used to pounce on people's backs and start swinging when she got upset.

The fellow tells me the cougar came to Vermont in a motorhome, while most of the members rode their bikes up.

The club was camping at Stub's and had chained the cougar up under the deck so she could be cool in the shade and out of sight while they ran errands.

They hadn't counted on a screaming little girl jumping up and down within reach of the chained panther.

To the cat, that child must have sounded like a big mouse and easy lunch, I'm thinking. Instinct kicked in.

It was a near deadly combination.

"I'm going to have to take your cougar," I tell the fellow. "It attacked a child here an hour or so ago. She's at the hospital. This cat has to be quarantined. Has it had a rabies shot?"

The fellow looks stunned and a red flush comes into his cheeks. He grips the chain tighter in his fist and pulls the panther closer to his side.

He makes it clear he doesn't want to turn the cat over to me.

"She's a pet. She likes people. She was just playing," he says.

"It doesn't matter. It's the law. I have to take her with me," I tell him.

"What are you gonna do with her?" he asks. It's clear he's thinking about fighting me. If the cat joins in any fracas, that would be an unforgettable tangle.

"I'm going to take her to a vet where she will be quarantined to make sure she's not sick. It would be the same as if this was a dog bite and the owner can't show me proof of a rabies vaccination," I tell him.

I can see the fellow weighing his choices. He's thinking how fast he can get his biker buddies here to help him and then how fast they can fold their tents, pile into that motor home and ride south, out of Vermont.

I try to clarify the situation for him.

"You and your club could be in a lot of trouble here. Why don't you just make this easier for the cat and for me and help me load her into the cage in the back of my truck?"

He's still thinking.

"If you try and stop me, you're going to jail."

I knew Stub had all the information on this club through their registration at the campground. I wanted to get the cougar in my truck and out of there as quickly as I could, before more bikers showed up and maybe wanted to start a fight over their mascot.

The cougar is eager to get moving, too. She's rubbing her head along the fellow's leg—from his pant pockets to his boot heels—like cats do.

She's so strong she's making this 225 pound fellow's knees buckle—rocking his whole body from side to side as she bangs her head into him over and over.

He looks down at the cat and says, "Okay," reluctantly.

I size up the cat. She's a good eight feet long from her nose to the tip of her tail. I'm not looking forward to trying to fit her in the cage in back of my truck alone.

"My truck is right out front. Head that way," I say, "and I'll follow you."

I have him go first so my back isn't to the cat or the man. I don't trust either of them.

I open the tailgate, pull the cage forward, pop open the door, and with a little encouragement from the biker, she jumps up effortlessly, ducks her head and strolls inside the cage.

The fellow unwraps the chain from his hand and it falls to the truck bed with a clatter as the cat lies down and begins to lick her paws.

I thank the fellow for his cooperation and let him know someone will be in touch with him a little later.

The sun is climbing into the sky and I want

to get the cat to a veterinarian as quickly as possible.

I realize I may need some help getting her out of the cage. As I leave Stub's, I radio the Dispatcher and ask her to call my friend and deputy, Art Chase of Hardwick, to ask if he's available to assist me.

I get a 10-4, and swing over to Art's house to pick him up on my way to St. Johnsbury.

"Come look at what I have in the back of the truck," I say to Art before we head out.

I lift up the truck cap and Art's eyes about pop out of his head. "Holy smokes! A live catamount? Are you serious? Where? What?"

Art is tongue tied.

"Jump in the truck and I'll tell you the story. I've got to get her to Doc Stetson's to be quarantined."

Art climbs in and I tell him the story. We're concerned for the child, but we appreciate what this animal represents, too.

"She's a beauty," Art says and I nod in agreement.

When we pull up to Doc Stetson's I quickly realize I've got a little problem: how to get the cat into his office building.

His office is close to the St. Johnsbury Academy and even though school is out right now, there are people around and this cat can cover a lot of ground fast.

The last thing I want is for this beast to get loose on me and run down Main Street.

I pop the truck cap and the cougar immediately jumps up and starts pawing the cage door. She hooks a claw the size of a butcher shop meat hook over the door latch and kinda jiggles it.

It's very clear she's tired of being caged and wants out.

Problem is, I don't have a fenced in yard for her to run in. She doesn't know me at all. I don't see opening that cage door and picking up her chain and trying to walk her into the vet's office as a good choice.

So, I try another idea.

"Art, we're going to have to carry this cage, with the cat inside, into Doc's," I say. "That means we'd going to have to watch our fingers. There's gloves in the cab. Grab a couple pairs and let's try this, okay?"

Art nods and goes to the front of the vehicle to search inside.

Suddenly, the thrill of having a live cougar in

the truck is gone. Now, it strikes me that we have a muscled monster here—and we could get torn up and bit bad, maybe even killed, if this cat takes a sudden dislike to us.

And if she gets loose, it could be a real disaster.

Art comes back with leather gloves for both of us.

"I'll take the front of the cage and you take the back. If we can keep her balanced and level, she should be okay with it. But watch your hands and don't get your body close to that cage," I warn him.

Art nods and we slide the cage forward and work to hustle her towards the vet's door, 100 feet or so from the parking lot.

But about 25 feet from the office door, I see this plan is not going to work.

The cage is a good foot wider than the front door. No way do I want to be turning and twisting this lightly built metal cage—rocking and rolling the cougar and angering her—to maybe make it through the door.

"Stop! Stop, Art," I say. "Set her down. We've got a problem."

The two of us lower the cage to the front lawn. "She's gonna have to come out of the cage and be led in," I say. "The cage is just too wide. Wait right here. I want to go warn Doc."

I walk into the office and once I explain what I intend to bring inside—and folks look through the curtains to confirm I'm not joking—the waiting room, reception and billing department clears out faster than if I yelled, "Fire!"

All except for Doc. He's got a grin on his face the size of Kansas. He can't wait to meet her.

I prop the office door open, walk out to Art and say, "I'm going to open the cage door and grab ahold of her chain, but if she starts to move out fast, you may have to grab ahold of the chain, too. She's powerful."

Art hunkers down and perches on the pavement like a center on the football team, ready for any move the cat makes. We hope.

I lift the latch on the cage door and sure enough, the cat leaps. Actually, explodes is more like it.

I've got ahold of her chain, but it runs through the cage like greased lightening. The cat moves out so fast, the cage bounces along behind.

I'm running to keep up with her as best I can. Art is behind me, trying to dodge the bouncing cage, and the two of us and the cage—we're like gold charms on a belly dancer's belt. We're getting tossed every which way.

I've held onto a lot of big dogs before—from St. Bernards to Great Danes.

The power of this panther has 'em all beat by a factor of at least 10. It's like trying to stop Zenyatta out of the starting gate.

I lean back and dig in my heels and the chain tightens around my hand like it's about to cut in two.

Not a dent in her stride.

The only good part of this tow is I know this cat won't kick me like a moose might. But if she turns around or gets me on the ground, I'll be in real trouble.

Art's trying to dodge the cage and keep it from beating us both to death as it bounces behind the panther like a tractor tire being pulled by a charging 1,200 pound bull.

I realize we need to distract this cat or she'll get away from us.

"Grab her tail!" I shout to Art.

The cat's tail is the only lever we have that might momentarily distract her.

It's a risky move, because once we get ahold of her tail, what then? Do you declare victory just before you're clawed to pieces?

And grabbing ahold of her tail isn't as easy as it sounds either, because she is whipping it back and forth like a high pressure fire hose. She's not happy we are trying to slow her down.

Art leaps, misses, runs another couple steps,
springs and dives. This time he catches her
tail, wraps both hands around it, leans back
and pulls.

It slows her down all right. In an instant she
spins and hisses at the two of us.

I don't know which is worse—her trying to get
away or the warning she's giving us now that
she'll attack if we don't let go.

I look up and see we're only 20 feet from Doc
Stetson's front door. I've still got the chain.
I think I can use the cage as a kind of shield
if she comes after me or Art.

I give the chain a hard yank like I am
trying to get a bull to turn. I'm showing the
panther the office door in hopes she will see it
as a safe haven against these nutty fellows—
like a house cat would see a closet, as a place
to hide.

Art drops her tail, waiting. My arms are aching
and I can't feel my hand because she has pulled
the chain so tight.

"Come on, girl," I mutter under my breath.
If she gets an itch to run down St. J's Main
Street with me in tow, this could be bad.

I'm hoping her nose tells her there's a pack of
bloodhounds living in the neighborhood and she
ought to find a place to hide again.

Maybe the open door made Doc's place look like home. Maybe she expected to find a bowl of milk inside waiting. I've got no idea. But we got real lucky and she ran up the steps and slipped inside like a cat that hates the rain and wants a quiet, dry haven.

I trot after her and kick the door shut with my back foot. The noise makes the cat look at me. Her nose is up and she's sniffing the air. I spy a big bag of cat chow in the waiting room to my left. Most veterinarian's offices recommend and sell one brand or another.

Thinking, "maybe I can charm the beast with food," I reach over and grab a bag, tear it open and start imitating the sing song voice of the biker an hour or so ago.

"Come on, kitty. Lunch time. Here you go. Dinner. Hungry, girl?"

The cat turns and looks at me and lowers her head and tail and starts coming at me.

I've got one hand on my revolver and the other on the bag out in front of me with the chain beneath. I let some cat chow fall to the floor and step back. She walks over and lowers her body as big cats do—like they are doing push ups—and laps up and crunches down about a quart of the crunchy kitty chow.

I'm hoping she doesn't think this is just an appetizer and I'm the main course.

I decide I'm on to something and take my hand off the pistol butt and offer her more food. She crunches the second pile down and when she stands up, she slams her head onto my leg like she did with the biker earlier.

I guess she was hungry. That might have had something to do with her going after that girl.

I yell to Doc, who tells me how to get Carla into a bigger cage in the back.

After more food and some water, I've got a calmer cat slinking beside me. Once she's safely inside a bigger cage, Art and Doc Stetson join me.

All three of us are still unable to believe our eyes.

But the bigger question is, now what do we do with her?

I follow protocol and ask Doc to watch the cat for 10 days for any sign of illness. Our number one concern is rabies, of course. I borrow an office phone, call Waterbury and let my bosses know what I've got here.

I have to trust the higher ups in the Department to handle the cat's fate.

Lucky for Carla, in the century that's passed since the Barnard catamount was killed, people's attitudes about her species have changed dramatically. Once she shows no sign of illness, calls go out to various zoos and big cat rescues all over the country, trying to find her a permanent home.

I go back on the road and respond to new calls every day.

But through the grapevine, I hear the little girl the lion pounced on had no serious injuries. The collar on that life vest likely saved her.

Whether the cat just wanted to wrestle the child to the ground like she probably played with the bikers that had raised her from a kitten—or whether Carla really intended to kill the child—we'll never know.

Carla quickly became a favorite at Doc Stetson's. She was a charmer. She liked to butt her head right up against the dog run to beg for head scratches and roll on her back with all four feet up in the air like a giant house cat. She even purred.

But it just wasn't safe to take her up on her invitations. Even some house cats will pretend they want their belly rubbed and when you go to pet them, they will kick, scratch and bite as if to take your arm off.

Mother Nature had made Carla too big and powerful a wildcat to ever be domesticated. Doc made it clear no one was to handle or feed her but him. And he made certain to have someone outside the cage, ready to call for help if he got in trouble.

The beautiful beast deserved better.

When her quarantine period passed and she showed no signs of sickness, it was time to find a new home for her.

The Department finally struck gold with a call to the marketing department of the Ford Motor Company. The auto giant had the Mercury Cougar in their lineup at the time and live cougars were a part of that advertising campaign. Cougars were used not just in the television ads but for car shows as well.

It just so happened the tour was coming north out of Boston through the White River Junction area. And that's where Carla was dropped off a few weeks later.

She got a home with experts who knew how to keep her happy, room to roam when she wasn't working and even the chance to see other cougars.

And Art and I got bragging rights to a true story of wrestling a live catamount in the Green Mountains that—so far—no one alive can match.

"If this woodchuck lands on a vehicle below, the shock could cause a driver to swerve and slam on the brakes and result in a massive pile up."

Chuck Chase

Contributed by Robert Rooks

Some of a warden's biggest wildlife challenges occur not in the woods, but in suburbia—when humans and wildlife collide. And it isn't always the image Hollywood gives you either—of a valiant warden desperately poking a rotten tree limb at a bear about to pounce on a child.

Nope. A lot more often it's the little wild guys that test your mettle: skunks, raccoons, woodchucks, opossum, snakes and the like.

These little guys can be fast and their moves can be tough to predict. Worse, when dealing with them in town a warden often has an audience.

I was in the Williston barracks chasing paperwork around my desk when I got the call.

It was August. We'd had a series of hot, muggy days and on the drive into work I heard the guys over at the Fairbanks Museum promise their Vermont Public Radio audience more of the same today: high 90s with high humidity.

So, as much as I love to work outdoors, I

wasn't exactly heartbroken to be stuck in air conditioned splendor sorting through a big stack of reports I had to review.

I'd been in Waterbury earlier in the day to meet with the Commissioner, so I was wearing my dress uniform. I was buttoned up from the tip of my boots to my chin in wool—summer weight wool—but still wool.

I hadn't brought a change of uniform with me, because I was confident I wouldn't be called out this day.

Wrong.

I was on my third cup of coffee and the clock on the wall said it was around 1 pm, when a complaint came in through the Dispatcher, who patched it over to my desk.

It was a young woman on a cell phone talking fast. It was a bad connection and some words dropped as she talked to me.

But even with losing big chunks of her call, I could hear fear in her voice.

She said something about preschoolers, a picnic and a woodchuck acting strangely on a bridge over in the north end of Burlington.

And one word that came through loud and clear was "bite."

When you pair up words like woodchuck, children and bite, you really get a warden's attention.

I had to get out there fast.

Woodchucks aren't known for being aggressive or ferocious. So, it's pretty strange one would attack a child. Their primary defense is to duck and run into their den.

They are in the marmot family, along with their western cousins, prairie dogs. And while farmers aren't fond of them, chucks have actually been found to play a role in aerating soil and, of course, they are a favorite meal for many predators.

While our department was mostly focused on the possibility of raccoons spreading rabies, it certainly was not out of the realm of possibility that a woodchuck could have contracted the disease.

One of the symptoms a rabies infected wild animal may exhibit is losing its fear of humans. A normally shy woodchuck acting aggressively and biting someone fit that symptom precisely.

I jumped out of my chair, let the folks in the office know I was taking this call, grabbed my hat and ran to my truck.

The second I opened the door to the parking lot a blast of heat and humidity engulfed me.

It was like entering a sauna. I felt beads of sweat forming on my forehead before I even opened the truck door.

I flipped on the blue lights and headed north on I-89, parting the cars headed to Burlington like Charleston Heston playing Moses.

I was on the scene in about 20 minutes.

I expected to be joining police cars or maybe see a rescue vehicle.

But all I saw were toddlers jumping and yelling and screaming and pointing towards a foot bridge, along with several hand wringing young ladies, who were in charge.

A young woman ran up to greet me as I stepped out of the truck. "That's him over there," she said with eyes wide and turning to point at the concrete bridge's footpath.

I squinted under my cap against the waves of heat rising up like a mirage. I saw a furry football hunkered down in the middle of the span.

"Okay," I nodded. "Keep everyone far away, please."

I had all kinds of questions I wanted to ask, but I didn't have time for a discussion.

If the critter took off and I lost him, the child or

children whom he had bitten were in for a series of rabies shots. You don't mess around with any animal bite, especially that of a wild animal.

I needed to get the chuck before I could take the time to get some answers.

But with a quick look at the surroundings, I realized this was not going to be an easy catch and dispatch.

Not only was the bridge concrete and steel— which could send a bullet ricocheting wildly— but beneath this span was a busy four lane highway, running north and south.

I couldn't risk firing my pistol here. I was going to have to use a catch pole to get this animal.

The tool isn't much more than pole with a noose at one end and a hank of rope running through to your hand to pull it tight.

Get the noose around the animal's neck, pull fast on the slider and you've caught the critter. It keeps them at arm's length, so they can't come at you and bite.

Of course, it helps if the animal actually has a neck. Woodchucks are seriously challenged in that area. They're little sumo wrestlers—all head and body and no neck.

So, I knew getting a noose around the rodent's neck and pulling it tight was likely to be a challenge—kinda like tightening a noose around a football.

But it was the only way I could go here. I could try a net, but odds were the animal would chew right through the mesh.

So, I dug around in the back of my truck, found the pole handle, shook all the gear off that was covering it, and trotted to the edge of the bridge with the eyes of a dozen kids and their teachers watching my every move.

The sweat was already spitting up underneath my cap.

Out of the corner of my eye I saw all these toddlers and their chaperones following my every move.

Well, I couldn't let that stop me.

In the back of my mind, I was thinking a rescue squad must have already taken the child away that was bitten or maybe the parent or another teacher had driven the child to a hospital emergency room.

It had taken me a lot longer to get there than it would have city police. I figured I was the clean up crew. Wardens often are.

I decided to approach the woodchuck at a slow and steady walk—to get as close as I could without agitating him.

I needed to get within eight feet or so before I could lower the noose. Running up on him would most likely trigger his fight or flight response. Trying to sneak up might do the same.

I wanted to avoid making him bolt.

I held the catch pole in my right hand, erect and close to my side, sorta hiding it.

I was doing pretty well for the first 25 feet.

As I approached the animal, I also took a good, hard look at his condition.

He looked to be in good weight, probably two to three years old, with a shiny coat—a mix of brown and black hair with some silver tips.

He was facing out towards the traffic beneath us, sitting motionless, still as a statue as prey animals can do.

Trying to hide in broad daylight, I guessed.

I could only see half of his furry face—one eye and a nostril and part of his mouth. But I didn't see a sickly dullness in his eye or any discharge from his nose or drool below his furry chin.

He looked healthy but frozen in place—in the wrong place.

But that didn't mean he wasn't infected with

some disease and dangerous. He had bitten
a child, so it was case closed—he was coming
with me.

But I soon learned that catching a woodchuck
isn't as easy as it sounds.

I got to within 15 feet of the animal, just two
or three slow steps from lowering the tip of the
catchpole, when he showed me he had feet.

He stood up to his full height of about 10 inches
and scooted, with his stub brush tail waving
goodbye.

Well, I couldn't let him escape. So, I kicked into
high gear and took off after him.

I'm six feet tall, racing an eight pound rodent
with legs maybe four inches long.

You'd figure this would be no contest.

I should win hands down.

You'd be wrong.

Truth be told, that fat rat could really move.
He was the Pete Rose of rodents, a furry Charlie
Hustle.

I dug in—as much as I could dig—into cement
—leaned forward and started pumping my arms
up and down like the coach had taught us back
in high school track class.

I lowered the noose, but he dodged it like a
tiny tight end.

I tried again and again, but I only tickled his
nose once.

I realized I wasn't going to have any chance
of noosing him until he was stopped.

But what could I use as a wall?

I decided my boots would have to suffice.

I ran past him about 10 feet, jumped and
planted my boots in his path, sideways,
like I wanted to keep water from running
through.

It worked. He saw black in his path, stopped
dead and sat there staring, a foot from my toes
trying to figure out what to do.

I figured I've got him now. I just have to hope
he doesn't look up as I lower the noose in front
of his head.

I'm doing my best not to breathe or so much
as blink. But I can't stop the sweat from
dripping off me.

The chuck crouches still as a cottontail in
tall grass hoping the fox will walk on by him.
This animal doesn't so much as blink.

I lower the noose slowly, like I'm lowering a

flag. I'm seconds away from nabbing him and trying not to smile.

The loop is just six inches away from his head when the muscled marmot spins, his claws clatter, and he streaks back towards the school group.

Not good.

What could I do?

I rise up onto my toes and chase after him again.

The chuck was really going for it now—a furred flounder in fast forward. His loose brown skin kinda floated above the bridge like a brown hovercraft.

I needed to turn on the turbo. I dropped down a good six inches in height and moved out like a racehorse that understood he was headed to the glue factory if he didn't win this race.

Truth be told, the woods rat had tremendous talent as a sprinter. The better to escape a fox, I suppose.

I reach the catchpole way out in front of me again, thinking I might get lucky with the noose.

But I'm like a man with a blindfold swinging at a piñata. I can't make the grab.

I decide to use my feet to set up another road block.

I leap up and over him—like a kid playing Ninja warrior. I plant my feet sideways and yell "HA!" to scare him into frozen bunny mode once again.

It works.

He slams on the brakes like he's a battery operated toy and I had hit the off switch.

He's hunkered down, black eyes staring straight ahead. He was so short he couldn't see past my bootlaces.

His sides heave as he works to catch a breath. I'm doing the same.

There's a river of sweat dripping into and stinging my eyes. My shirt is sticking to my back.

I wanted to call, "Time out!" bend over and ask the coach to take me out of the game for 10 minutes. But there's no second string and no bench on this job.

I also wanted badly to reach for my pistol, shoot the woodchuck, noose him, bag him and drive him to the lab for testing.

But I couldn't chance a shot on concrete. Ricochets can kill.

As I'm trying to get my breath, I have a feeling the chuck is doing the same and we're thinking the same thing: "Now what?"

Once again, the furry flivver made the next move.

He spun like a world champion barrel horse and took off again towards the opposite end of the bridge.

Worse, I heard cheering and some applause from the kids behind me.

I couldn't tell if the crowd was cheering for me or my new racing partner. I had a sense the toddlers might be starting to place bets on who would win.

I shook my head, gritted my teeth and prayed no one in the crowd had a video camera and off I went again—chasing the fast rat.

I'm wondering if maybe he might just do me a big favor and keel over? He sure isn't acting very sick.

It wasn't looking good for my noose plan.

I think, maybe I can step on his tail and stop him in his tracks. So I reach out with my right foot and step big at his backside trying to catch that brushy tail.

No dice.

It was like trying to land a boot on a flying
egg beater.

I'm running out of options and patience.

I decide smacking him hard with the catchpole
is my only hope.

I run up alongside him and swing big.

But this guy's beady eyes are made for
spotting hawks and owls swooping at him
from above. He dodges and I miss, sending
a reverberation up the pole and into my arm
like I had stuck my hand in an electrical outlet.

I grit my teeth, keep running and try again and
again.

THWACK! THWACK! THWACK!

I don't hit him, but I scare him big time.

He jumps high and to the left, twists like a tuna
on a hook, lands on his ribs and slides under
the bottom rail of the bridge.

He disappears over the side!

I can't believe my eyes. I slam on the brakes
and almost fall down on my back pockets.

Now, in addition to a child having to get rabies
vaccinations, we might be looking at mass
casualties and property damage.

If this woodchuck lands on a vehicle below, the shock could cause a driver to swerve and slam on the brakes and result in a massive pile up.

I cringe.

I listen for the sound of brakes locking up, truck horns blaring, bumpers slamming, sheet metal folding and glass shattering.

My heart—which had been beating a healthy rate after sprinting with the woodchuck—now feels like it has stopped beating entirely.

I shut my eyes and listen for the sounds of a demolition derby beneath me.

But after five seconds—nothing.

I open my eyes and run to the side of the bridge and look. Traffic is still flowing.

There's no brown body on the asphalt.

But where is he?

Suddenly, movement low and to the right catches my eye.

I gasp.

It's the woodchuck hanging by his front claws onto the metal drip edge affixed to the side of the bridge.

My immediate instinct is to throw myself
onto the cement and reach out and give him
a hand—like he's a buddy who's fallen off a
trail onto a narrow ledge.

But of course, that couldn't happen. He'll
panic and let go or bite me or both.

Now, what do I do?

I do the only thing I can do—which is back
up and start praying.

Will he be able to pull himself back onto the
bridge?

How strong is a woodchuck?

He wriggles his head side to side. I see his
back legs moving up and down. I can't hear
above the din of the traffic below, but I see
he's scratching his back claws on the concrete,
trying to get a toehold.

I am rooting for this woodchuck to pull himself
back up onto the deck as if my career depends
on it.

Because it might.

I can't tell you how long the woodchuck
struggled. The world kind of stands still when
you are a witness to a calamity.

I honestly didn't think he had a chance.

I figured he would tire, a front paw would slip
and it would be Sayonara, Rabid Rodent.

I underestimated him.

I saw a hip rise up and realized he'd caught a
back foot on something solid. He hung there a
split second, resting.

Then his head bobbed up an inch above the rail
and a quivering, shuddering shoulder followed
as he got a toehold with the other hind leg.

My mouth fell open. This was one strong,
determined beast.

He folded himself in half like a caterpillar
hunches up on a leaf, and wriggled his body
up onto the bridge.

I wanted to applaud. Not many humans could
do what he'd just done.

I was feeling a little bad about how this all had
to end.

I still had to catch and kill him.

I took a big step backwards to let him catch
his breath. It wasn't that I was playing by
Marquess of Queensbury rules. I just needed
for the chuck to waddle back onto the main
footpath and away from the railing before I
took another run at nabbing him.

I didn't think either one of us could take another cliffhanger. One or both of us might have a fatal heart attack.

It looked like he was frozen up again like when I first found him.

I didn't have time to wait him out. I was soaked with sweat and wanting to wrap this up.

I walked to the railing, put the pole over the side and waved it up and down just behind his rump. That got him to run forward and onto the main footpath again.

We were back to where we started a good half hour and a lot of water weight ago.

The only good news was the crowd of teachers and preschoolers had thinned out considerably.

Standing there panting, salty sweat running like water into my eyes, stinging and blinding me, I tried to think of what his dear mama might have said to get him to move.

What would Mama Chuck say?

Darned if I knew.

All I had heard from him so far was chattering teeth and an alarm whistle—both of which appear to trigger a big scoot, not the sidewalk saunter I needed.

I sighed and decided to go with what I knew—which was more bovine and cowboy than woodchuck talk.

I figured I had nothing to lose.

"Come on, Chuck. Giddy up," I said. "Let's go."

My voice prompted a little shudder in him—a ripple from his head to this tail and his head came up an inch or two.

He didn't move, but he was definitely listening.

"Come, on Chuckie, let's go home," I said with a touch more urgency. I took a step forward.

Maybe my marmot mate was so exhausted from our runs that a wobbly waddle was all he had left.

Maybe he'd decided if he was still alive at this stage, I was just a pest but not a predator.

Maybe he understood English and I should have introduced myself in the first place and saved myself a whole lot of shin splints from racing him on this concrete bridge.

He rose up on all four paws as if he was a brown mutt of some sort and just tall enough to clear his belly from the street—and began waddling forward—like he understood me perfectly.

I took another smooth step and then another. He was was headed right where I wanted him —off the bridge.

It was going so well there for 30 feet or so a bystander might have thought I was walking a new breed of dog.

He was just about off the bridge and I was reaching for my pistol when I hear a woman scream and shout, "What are you doing?"

I hadn't expected it and neither did the chuck.

We both jumped. He hung a sharp left, ducking beneath the concrete and steel.

My opportunity to shoot evaporated. Now, I was going to have to go underneath the bridge deck to search for him.

I wanted to scream. But I bit my tongue. This job is as much about the public as it is about the wildlife, I told myself.

I turned to face the screamer and explain the situation.

"This woodchuck bit a child. It's brain has to be tested for rabies. I have to kill it. You need to step back and let me do my job. Now," I said.

"But he didn't bite anyone," she said indignantly.

I was crouched, climbing beneath the bridge, looking for a den hole and faced with a whole new challenge—smoking him out when I heard her.

I spun around, turned and poked my head back out into the light and said, "What did you just say?"

"That woodchuck didn't bite anyone," she said again. And she looked at me like I was nuts.

I slid my revolver back into its holster, took a deep breath and looked hard at the young woman.

"I came out here because I got a call saying a child had been bitten by a woodchuck," I said —sweat dripping off me like I was in a sauna.

"I'm the one who called," she said. "What I said was there was a woodchuck on the bridge and the children and I were worried about him because he was just sitting there and that he *might bite* a child. But he didn't. He just stayed frozen in the middle of the bridge until you showed up and started to chase him."

"Are you telling me nobody was bitten?" I said again—just to be clear.

"No, I mean, yes," she said. "I mean, that woodchuck didn't bite anyone. The children and I were worried about him sitting there in the middle of the bridge. It's so hot and all. We didn't know what to do, so I called the police."

That's when it struck me that what I had been racing was a woodchuck who went for a stroll and found himself on concrete, looking over a bridge at traffic.

It was so foreign to a creature used to hiding in tall grass and dandelions, he froze in terror.

He was like a cat that runs up a tree and then is so scared it takes a fire department ladder to bring it down.

An agoraphobic woodchuck.

"Excuse me, Miss," I said. I'm not taking her word for this. I decide to make certain she's telling me the truth.

I walked to my truck and called the Dispatcher.

Had anyone been admitted for an animal bite in the Burlington area? Had police been called here earlier?

The call comes back about seven minutes later—no reports of any animal bites or police or rescue having been called to this location.

The young woman is still waiting for me in the shade of a crab apple tree.

I take a deep breath, then step out of the truck.

"Is he going to be all right?" she asks.

"Who are you talking about?" I ask her.

"The woodchuck," she said. "Is he going to be all right?"

I'm a mess. My head is pounding. I'm dying for a pitcher of ice cold water.

I imagine the woodchuck deep in his cool earthen den, his feet—sore from racing me —soaking in a bath of cool Epsom salts, sipping an ice cold strawberry Daiquiri through a straw and catching the bottom of today's Red Sox double header on Chuck TV.

I might have been hallucinating a little from the heat.

This young lady doesn't think to apologize for dragging me out in the middle of the day to rescue a woodchuck from a panic attack or even ask if I'm all right.

This is where the public relations piece of the job comes in.

I bite the inside of my cheek, paste a crooked smile on my face and say as calmly as I can, "I'm sure he'll be fine. Just, please, leave the animal alone. Leave all wildlife alone. Teach the children to leave them all alone."

"Oh, well that's good to know. I'm sure the children will be happy to hear he will be fine," she says, adding, "Thank you for getting him out of the hot sun."

She turns and heads to her car.

I wait until she drives away. She's the type that might decide to come back and leave him some treats or something.

Once she's outta there, I head back to Williston, shaking my head.

Like we wardens often say, it's not always the animals. Sometimes, it's the people that are the problem.

"All I could think of was, maybe they
had opened their cages and torn the
place apart, then went back inside
and latched the doors when they
heard us coming."

MONKEY MUDDLE

CONTRIBUTED BY ROBERT ROOKS

We got a tip that a family down in southern Vermont was keeping monkeys as pets.

Monkeys are smart, strong, fast and unpredictable. They also carry a long list of diseases that can be deadly to humans. It is illegal to possess them in Vermont.

Before we could seize the animals, we had to have a place to put them. Finding the animals a new home became my job. I spent days on the phone, calling all over the country, trying to find a zoo or some other facility that would accept them.

I finally located a rescue organization in Ohio. The manager said she would take the monkeys as long as a licensed veterinarian examined them and certified they were in good health.

I thanked the woman profusely and asked her to fax me the paperwork she wanted signed. I told her I'd get the animals to her door in just a few days.

I didn't want to give her time to change her mind.

Then I called the wardens, Dave and Ed, and authorized them to seize the animals and bring them up to headquarters as quickly as they could.

The guys had been conducting surveillance on the home—which was set way back on a dead end road in the woods—on and off for a few weeks.

They had developed a pretty good idea of the family's routine.

It was late afternoon when they knocked on the front door of the house.

While two wardens talked to the husband and wife and explained Vermont law and the public health threat their pets posed, a third warden, Jake, moved quickly to pick up the caged monkeys from a back bedroom, scoot them out the back door and into the open hatch of a waiting truck.

The fellows told me later their biggest challenge was not throwing up. The monkey stink inside the bedroom was beyond anything they'd ever encountered.

Think years of body odor and bad teeth, combined with feces and urine and rotten bananas and other fruit, combined with lettuce

and carrots and who knows—all mixed together
in a stifling room heated to better than 80
degrees.

The family might have had real affection for
their animals, but the quality of life these
simians were living was less than humane.

Despite noisy protests from the owners and
the monkeys, the wardens made it out of the
driveway without any real problems—except for
some retching and watery eyes.

Dave and Ed left Jacob behind and the truck
was driven north to Waterbury, where I was
pacing and watching the clock.

My plan was to have a veterinarian examine
the animals early the next morning and then
have Dave drive them to Ohio.

But where to keep the monkeys overnight?

After a lot of thought, I decided on the basement
armory of our Waterbury office. The solid steel
door was always locked and only a few people
had access. I was one of them.

True, the armory contained dozens of shotguns,
pistols, rifles and cases of ammo and other
supplies.

But I was fairly confident these animals hadn't
learned to shoot and we weren't going to let
them out of their cages.

In terms of protecting the public, I thought it was the best choice.

It was a little after 6 pm when the fellows pulled up in the truck. All was quiet in the back until Ed opened the truck cap.

The trio started screaming like Cheetah in an old Johnny Weissmuller movie, baring their teeth and reaching out like furious little King Kongs wanting to get a piece of us.

I leaned in under the cap to take a closer look and was immediately knocked back on my heels, like I'd been hit in the face with a stink bomb.

If ever there was a time to use gas masks and ear plugs, this would have been it.

Maybe the screaming was their way of demanding a hot bath and a bar of soap?

I have to think they didn't much like the way they smelled either.

Worse, it looked like someone had used the truck bed as a kennel for three big dogs and a couple ponies for a week. Their filth was everywhere. These apes had even managed to spray urine onto the windows and ceiling.

As I reached into the truck bed to help the guys grab the cages, I began to gag.

I thought I was going to lose my lunch.
I motioned with my left arm towards the
building's back door, got a hand on the cage
handle and held my breath.

The three of us—cages in hand—ran as fast as
we could with our faces red, cheeks puffed out,
trying to hold our collective breath.

I suppose we looked a little odd to anyone
standing upwind, like we were practicing to
become pearl divers or something.

If there were an annual award within the
Department for "overcoming stink beyond the
call of duty" these men would have won hands
down.

We trotted down the stairs until we reached
the armory. I unlocked the door and opened it
wide. We scooted the cages inside and set them
down on the concrete floor.

The animals reached for our pant legs, tried to
grab our shirt cuffs. It sounds cute, but it was
really quite dangerous.

One good handful of fabric and a solid yank to
the side of a cage and they could bite or scratch
us with their long filthy fingernails. Any break
in the skin or even just being spit on by these
simians could result in a serious infection or
debilitating illness.

I'd bought bananas, grapes and bottles of

water for them earlier in the day and had the bags of goodies waiting in a corner. I took about half the food along with a bottle of water for each of them and dropped it into their cages. The food quieted them down a bit. They stopped screeching and showing us their very impressive teeth and focused on the food instead.

I nodded to the guys, and together we slipped out of the armory. I locked the door behind us, and we climbed the stairs and went outside to witness a setting sun and a very filthy truck bed.

Ed found a garden hose and did his best to pressure wash the inside of the cap while Dave and I made plans for the next morning

"Fill that gas tank tonight and be back here at Oh Dark Thirty," I told him. "As soon as the vet signs the health papers for these monkeys, you are outta here."

Dave nodded and promised to be back before dawn.

It had been a struggle to find a veterinarian willing to come examine the animals. I'd made six or more calls and all of them told me they had no experience with exotic species, no time to assist or both. A few of them warned me of the danger of serious disease handling them.

I finally convinced a fellow in a solo practice

to come. After some hemming and hawing, he promised to arrive at 6 am.

The guys and I split up and I went home to a late supper and early bed.

I tossed and turned. I had a sense something or someone was out there trying to—forgive the pun—throw a monkey wrench into this operation.

By 4 am I decided to just get on over to the office and wait for the vet to arrive.

I grabbed a cup of coffee and a muffin at an all night coffee shop off I-89, and pulled in at the back of the building just as the first bird started calling.

I stopped short of going down to the armory to check on the monkeys. I didn't want them screaming. I'd wait for Dave.

Dave pulled in around 5 am.

"Got the truck gassed up?"

"Yes, sir."

"A couple meals packed?"

"Cooler in the back will last me a few days," he grinned.

"Lots of water?"

"Yes, sir."

"Bananas and grapes for the apes?" I teased him.

"I picked up a few more bunches on the way home last night. We're good there, too."

"Well, I guess now we just wait for the vet." I said. "Climb into my truck. He should be here any minute."

Dave slid into the cab and we chatted about not much while looking off down the driveway for headlights.

At 6:15 am there was still no sign of him.

This was not good. Hundreds of state employees' vehicles would be streaming onto the Waterbury complex within the hour. A few early birds were already taking the choice parking spots.

The whole point of scheduling the exam at 6 am was to minimize human exposure to these animals.

I felt my blood pressure rising. I had to get this operation moving.

"Dave, go on down to the armory and bring the cages up one at a time. The vet can do his exam in the back of the truck. We've got to get you on the road."

Dave had no more than closed the passenger door when my truck radio came to life. It was the Dispatcher telling me the vet would not be coming.

No further explanation was provided.

"10-4," I said and hung up before something inappropriate came out of my mouth.

I took a long deep breath and clenched my teeth. If ever I came close to behaving like one of the caged animals in the building behind me, this was it. I wanted to rip the steering wheel off the column.

When I regained my composure, I got back on the radio and politely asked the Dispatcher to patch me through to our Dr. Doolittle for a private conversation. I didn't want anyone listening in.

When the connection was made, I expressed my dismay at his failure to show in very clear language.

And I told him I was done begging and pleading.

"You gave me your word you would examine these monkeys at 6 am and you're now a half hour late. I am going to alert all available law enforcement to arrest you. You're coming one way or the other—now," I said.

He sputtered for a bit. But it worked.

He said he'd be at my door in a half hour.

I had just hung up when I saw Dave running empty handed towards the truck from my rear view window. The look on his face told me something was wrong.

"What now?" I muttered, and jumped out of the cab to intercept him.

"The monkeys!" he said breathlessly, bending over to catch his breath like a runner at the end of the Boston Marathon.

"What about them?" I asked, my mind racing as to what trouble they could cause.

"Mess, biiiiig mess," he said, still hunched over but beginning to catch his breath and straighten his back. "You gotta come see."

Dave turned and ran back towards the building, down the basement stairs into the armory with me on his heels.

We were two floors above the arms depot when the monkey smell in the stairwell began to hit me. I couldn't believe creatures so small could produce a stink that big.

It was a real possibility they might foul the air of this entire building and require an evacuation. Maybe I should be the one behind the wheel to Ohio. I had to get these animals out of here fast.

Dave tore open the door to the Armory, stepped back and let me look.

My mouth fell open—despite the stench—and I rocked back and forth on my heels unable to believe my eyes.

Rifles and shotguns were torn from their rests against the walls and scattered about the floor like toys. Boxes of shotgun shells and single cartridges had been chewed, torn and tossed.

Shells were lying everywhere—.22 shells and .357s were shining like copper pennies under the overhead lights.

Paper targets had been scattered about like someone had gone crazy in an office supply store.

And all of this was mashed together with some banana peels and squished grapes and water. Or were some of those wet spots monkey pee and a lot worse?

"How did they do this?" I said incredulously, looking at Dave. He's looking back at me shaking his head wondering the same thing.

They were still in their cages. All I could think of was, maybe they had opened their cages and torn the place apart, then went back inside and latched the doors when they heard us coming.

I felt the cup of coffee and muffin I had for

breakfast start to climb its way back into my throat. I blinked, swallowed hard and said, "I'll deal with it later. Let's get 'em into the truck."

Easier said than done.

I wasn't 100 percent certain these animals hadn't learned to load, aim and fire.

One was chewing on a 12 gauge shell and screaming at me while his other hand swung a .357 revolver back and forth in my direction.

The second one was literally spitting bullets at us—he had put a bunch of .22 short rim fire cartridges in his mouth and was aiming at us like a little brother with a jaw full of watermelon seeds.

The third one was dangerously close to actually loading a rifle. He had a bolt action Remington in his hands and had opened the chamber and was busy trying to find a shell that would fit from the hundreds spread willy nilly all over the floor.

It was only a matter of time before he was successful. That sent a chill down my spine.

I bent down and dove in low towards his cage and grabbed the Remington with both hands —one on the barrel and the other on the stock.

He screeched and jumped like a sprung coil spring inside his cage—moving his cage sideways a good two feet. He yanked the rifle in closer to him.

I knew that in a tug of war I might lose.
So, I twisted the muzzle up and away sharply.
That slammed the monkey's arms into the stiff panel cage wire and surprised him.

He let go.

I picked up the rifle, held it up to the light and peered into the chamber. In addition to his search for a cartridge that would fit, he had stuffed a couple grapes and a piece of banana down the barrel.

I set the Remington on an open rest against the wall and looked at my watch.

Last thing I needed was an excuse for the vet to show up and then take off saying we weren't there to meet him.

"Grab 'em, we got to go," I said to Dave, nodding my head at a cage while picking it up and running towards the door for the stairs.

"Shut the door behind us," I shouted as I trotted out the door.

I didn't want anyone to see the mess this troublemaking trio had left behind.

As soon as we picked up the cages, the screeching started and this time, it bounced off the stairwell to a near full office building. Workers were coming into the building to their desks likes bees to a hive.

Dave and I ran across the parking lot carrying the cages and grimacing. Up above us, the windows were filling with curious workers watching us load the monkeys into the truck bed.

We got 'em inside the truck, shut the tailgate and cap lid and waited for the vet to pull up.

A couple minutes later, we saw a big red truck roll in slowly towards us with some fancy storage on the back.

"That's gotta be our guy," I say. Dave and I walk over to greet him.

A stout, silver haired fellow pulls up about 10 feet away from where we are standing and steps out from his truck. He's wearing a scowl on his face like a plumber who's been called away from Thanksgiving dinner to fix a broken sewer pipe.

"They're right over here," I say, leading the way to the back of the truck. The vet grabs a bag from the front seat of his truck, reaches for a pen and follows me in silence to the back of our truck.

Dave pops the truck cap lid and lowers the tailgate.

Those monkeys take one look at the vet and they go bananas.

Maybe this vet smelled like some mortal enemy of theirs or maybe they just didn't like his looks. I don't know. But, for whatever reason, the monkeys went beyond the teeth baring screams we'd become accustomed to, and ratcheted up their fury to a totally flat out, King Kong koo koo krazy, rage.

Dave and I are standing next to the open tailgate of the truck cap waiting for the vet to give us some direction as to how he wants to proceed, and the next thing we know, the cages are rocking and leaping and flying across the steel truck bed straight at all our heads.

Six ugly hairy hands with creepy long nails are reaching for our throats!

The caged monkeys were moving like luge runners at Lake Placid.

I take a huge step back. The vet about trips over his feet trying to back pedal. His face is white and his eyes are huge, like he had just come face to face with a crocodile.

Dave saves the day by ducking down and throwing the tailgate up hard and fast. That sends the cages up into the air, like they'd hit a brick wall.

Then I reach down and slam the truck cap shut.

None of us can talk because the monkey screeching is eardrum splitting loud.

I motion everyone away from the transport truck back over to the vet's vehicle.

We all gravitate to the hood. The vet's on one side leaning over a fender, I'm on the opposite side and Dave is standing a couple steps from the grill with his eyes still trained on the truck cap.

We're all trying to catch our breath, like men who just dodged the Grim Reaper.

As I'm trying to decide what to do next, a light bulb goes off in my head. Suddenly, I know how these animals had torn the armory apart.

They had taught themselves to sit back in their cage with their knees drawn up to their chests and their arms wide grasping the cage wire tight on each side of their prison and then they throw themselves in whatever direction they wanted to go.

They literally hurl their bodies hard enough to propel the cage forward.

Smart. Very smart.

They didn't need to escape. They rocked and walked their prisons wherever they wanted to go. When they reached their destination, they just reached out and tore stuff apart.

Which is what they clearly intended to do to us.

Wow.

I look over at the vet. When he arrived a few minutes ago, he had a scowl on his face and the dragging steps of a bored bully on his way to the principal's office.

But now that he's come face to face with blood thirsty monsters, he appears to be an entirely different man.

He looked up at me from across the hood of his truck like a man eager to escape before the police showed up at an out of control street fight.

"Okay!" he shouted and stuck his hand out.

"Okay what?" I shouted back.

"Give me the papers!" he yelled back at me.

I reached into my coat pocket and handed him the health papers before he could change his mind. With trembling hands, I saw him pick up a pen and begin checking boxes and scribbling notes. He had the intensity of a man defusing a bomb in a burning building.

There were beads of perspiration on his brow.

I look over at Dave and he looks sideways at me but we don't say a word.

I'm certainly not going to insist these animals
be removed from their cages so the doctor can
take their pulse and temperature and check
their teeth and whatever else.

Within two minutes, the vet is giving the sheets
a final once over. He signs each page, then
stands up and slides the papers across the
hood at me and dives for the driver's door of
his truck.

Dave and I look at each other—stunned.
Is that it?

Once inside the truck, the big man turns on
the ignition, then rolls down his window just far
enough for me to hear what he has to say.

"I'm a year away from retirement," he shouts to
me from the safety of his truck cab.

I nod to let him know I can hear him above
the din.

"You get another monkey or a saber tooth tiger
or Komodo dragon or whatever the heck wild
animal, you call someone else. I'm done."

He rolls up his window and yanks the truck into
gear. I step back. He punches the gas so hard
stones fly up as he drives away.

I turn to Dave with the signed health papers
firmly in my hand. I finally see light at the end
of this very messy monkey muddle tunnel.

"Take these papers, lock 'em in the glove box, get in the truck and drive! Don't stop for anything. And no matter what, do NOT bring those monkeys back!" I order him.

"Yes, sir!" Dave says. He jumps in the cab and fishtails the rig out of the yard just a tiny bit to show me he's got the message.

I sigh and head down to the armory with rubber gloves, a mask and a mop bucket.

I spent hours cleaning up that mess. Dave called me at home later that night with the good news the screamers were now officially Buckeye State residents.

Six months later, I had another exotic pet situation. I called the grumpy veterinarian's office thinking he could help me out again. I figured he'd have gotten over his attitude by now. Maybe he just wasn't a morning person.

His phone was disconnected. I called another vet, trying to track him down. I learned he'd closed his practice and moved to Washington State.

Hadn't he heard of Sasquatch?

"I could feel her eyes drilling into me like an angry brain surgeon going through a nasty divorce."

Rememberin' Red
Don't Lose Him

CONTRIBUTED BY RICHARD HISLOP

Among wardens and folks that knew him, Red Hooper stories are handed down from generation to generation like Grandpa's favorite shotgun.

Red was a skilled outdoorsman, top shot, sugar maker and insightful Yankee whose words could clear a room of hot air like a February nor'easter blows in your cabin door.

He was also a Vermont fish and game warden for 40 years and a member of the Vermont Legislature for 18.

Just mention Red and the people who knew him—and many who didn't but have heard stories about the man from their parents and grandparents—will break into a chuckle and launch into a story about something Red said or did.

Born Franklin Hooper in 1904, early photos of Red show an auburn haired, raw boned young man with long legs, big ears and hands that make .22 shells look like celery seeds.

I don't claim to be an expert on the man. I was just one of many a warden trainee assigned to ride along with Red as part of my education back in1970, near the end of his career.

I'd already worked alongside a few other veteran wardens in southern Vermont. I had a good idea of what was expected of me.

So, it came as a bit of a surprise when I got special orders on this rotation.

"Don't lose Red," I was told.

"What do you mean?" I asked.

I'm thinking, "If anyone's going to get lost up in these woods of Johnson, Cambridge and thereabouts, it's gonna be me. Red knows the area like the back of his hand."

"I mean, don't let anything happen to the man," my supervisor said, staring me in the eye like the fate of the nation was at stake.

That kinda made me wonder if I was training to be a warden or maybe I'd signed into the Secret Service. But again, I don't say anything.

I just nod and say, "Yes, Sir."

I learned later Red had recently undergone surgery for a hernia he'd put up with for many years. He was supposed to take it easy. But a warden's job involves a lot of tugging, lifting, reaching, climbing, carrying and hauling. I wondered how this was going to work.

Before long I have a duffle bag and toothbrush stashed in a kinda depressing room a couple flights up creaky dark stairs over a Main Street store in Johnson, and I'm following Red Hooper around like a big puppy, listening and learning.

I found out the hard way that keeping up with Red wasn't going to be easy.

We were staking out a meadow up Crooks Road in Eden on a cold damp September night. Red had driven the cruiser way back up into the hills.

When it turned into a logging trail, he kept going another half mile. I knew more than to say anything, but I about tore the armrest off the cruiser passenger door more than once.

I was convinced the frame would get hung up or the gas or brake lines would bust and we'd be stranded.

But Red was an artful, if painfully slow, driver.

He finally pulled off into an abandoned farm field, backed the cruiser into the brush until the rear wheels spun and he couldn't go any farther, and shut her down—all lights off. It was a little after 9 pm. We rolled down the windows and sat there in silence. Waiting. Listening.

Within seconds, I can see my breath and in less

than half an hour, there's frost crawling up on the inside of the windshield.

Not a word from Red.

We sit for hours and do not see or hear anything remotely like a car or a truck or a human walking anywhere near us.

A little after 2 am, I'm so cold I think I might lose one or more toes or fingers and I'm having real trouble keeping my eyes open.

I finally screw up my courage and speak. "Uh, Red, it's close to 3 am. We haven't seen any sign of jacking here. You think maybe we might head back soon?"

Red lifts his chin. He nods slightly and says without any anger in his voice, "I'll take you home."

I am some relieved.

Red leans forward and turns the key in the ignition. He gets us out of the puckerbrush, and works the steering wheel back and forth to get us turned around back down the trail.

It is so frosty inside the windshield, we have to wait a few minutes until the car engine warms up and we can rub away at the glass.

But as soon as he'd cooked a half dollar-sized patch of frost off the inside of the windshield, Red pulls out onto the trail and we bump and bounce, shake and slam back down the logging trail.

I breathe a big sigh of relief when I am finally able to roll up my window and shut the bone chilling night air out. When real heat rolls out of the floor vents, 15 minutes into the ride, I begin to think I may keep my toes.

About 45 minutes later, Red pulls onto Main Street.

A street light shines yellow over a few inches of snow on the ground. There's not a soul in sight. Everyone is warm in their beds and it is my turn next.

I had my room key in my hand before I even stepped out of the cruiser.

"Thanks, Red. I'll catch a little shut eye and see you in a few hours," I say as I climb out of the cruiser and shut the passenger door.

I dash through the snow and trot with bleary eyes up the stairs, unlock the door to my room and don't even bother to turn on the light.

Heat and sleep are all I want.

I unlace my boots, kick them off one at a time so they skitter across the floor into the dark, lift the covers up on my bed just wide enough to let me crawl in and collapse.

Then I pull the blankets back over me tight as a cigar wrapper. I was out like a bad bulb in about a minute.

Pounding on the door wrecked my sweet slumber. I awoke with a start, looked around to see where I was, wiped the drool from my mouth, ran to the door, opened it and saw Babe —one of Red's two daughters—standing there and looking none too happy.

She skipped the small talk. "Where's my father?" she asks like I just stole her wallet.

"He's home," I say, stifling a yawn. I was trying to be polite, but I want badly to shut the door in her face and just fall back to bed.

"No, he's not," Babe says with equal doses of conviction and indignation.

My eyes had fallen shut again. I might be on my feet, but I was still asleep. Babe stamps her foot on the warped hallway hardwood to wake me up. I snap to attention, open my eyes wide and try harder to focus my eyes and brain.

"What time is it?" I ask in an attempt to get my bearings.

"It's seven—in the morning," she says with the inference that I was some kinda layabout for being in bed at this late hour of a new day. "Daddy isn't home."

It's clear she isn't going to leave without more information from me. I can't help it, I yawn big.

"We were on a stakeout and Red dropped me off

here about 4 am," I tell her. "He's gotta be home."

I'm trying to convince Babe and now, myself.

"Where else would he be?" I say out loud.

"He's not home," she says again, with the emphasis on the "not." Her shoulders are shaking in anger and her eyes are sparking like a welder's torch.

"It's your job to watch him," Babe says.
"YOU need to go find him," she declares.

I blink a couple more times trying to focus.

"Go find Daddy," she says again, stamping her other boot.

"Daddy?" my brain is searching its data banks. This woman isn't any relative of mine—is she?

Then all of a sudden, it registers big time where I am living and the job I have and who she's talking about.

"Holy smokes! I've lost Red!"

The top job I've been assigned and I may have blown it.

The ramifications quickly fly through my mind: I see my new career flaming out like a cheap Fourth of July sparkler, my wife and kids homeless and me—forever being known as the dope who let the "Legend" get hurt.

My head jerks back, my eyes fly open and I spin
into the room searching for the boots I kicked off
a few hours earlier.

I'm stumbling around the room like Boris Karloff
playing Frankenstein, my arms stretched out in
front of me, reaching for anything solid.

If something has happened to Red, I am in big
trouble. This is Franklin "Red" Hooper, for
Heaven's sake.

Losing him would be a mark of shame I could
never live down. I'd have to leave the state or
at least change my name if something bad has
happened to him.

I turn around and go looking for my boots.
I trip over them and pick up yesterday's socks.
Seconds later, boots on, I grab my gun belt,
my badge and room key, nod to Babe and say,
"Okay, let's go find him."

I ride with Babe to her home, where a quiet
but frantic search is launched. We make calls
to family and friends looking for Red—pulling
his pals away from their morning coffee,
Johnnycakes and sausage to ask as casually as
we can, if they've seen Red this morning.

After 15 minutes of calling Red's family and
friends and getting nowhere, I realize I am going
to have to make the call I really don't want to
make—the one that will strongly indicate I have
indeed lost my boss.

But with Babe staring at me across the table like a hungry wolf eyeing a lame ram, I got no choice.

I ring up the Dispatcher, identify myself, and ask her to radio 955—that's Red's call number—for his 10-20, his location.

Then I hang up the phone and sit there staring at it, because I sure as heck don't want to make eye contact with Babe.

I could feel her eyes drilling into me like an angry brain surgeon going through a nasty divorce.

I sit there across the kitchen table from Babe for five tortured minutes in total silence before the phone finally rings.

"955 is on a stake out," the Dispatcher says.

I'm stunned. "Stake out?" I say to myself. "Where? Why isn't he at home?"

She follows it up with, "955 says he will head home shortly and meet you there."

"10-4," I say and hang up the phone.

I feel my face going redder than red. I look up from the cradled phone to face Babe.

"Red's on his way home," I say.

"Where is he?" she asks.

"Back at the stake out," I say.

Babe looks at me like a chicken looks at a bug—just before it slams its beak down and swallows it whole. I'm stewing in a combination of embarrassment and awe.

Just because his trainee was cold and needed to go home and take a nap like a 6 year old kid, that didn't mean the veteran was going to quit.

Red had driven back up into the woods and kept vigil all by himself into the daylight hours —despite his orders to take it easy and the pain it had to cause him bumping over those ruts so soon after his surgery.

Worse, he's out working while I'm in a nice warm bed sleeping.

I grin a crooked, guilty smile at Babe.

She shakes her head like she's disgusted with me. If I'd had a tail I would have tucked it between my legs and hidden under the couch.

When Red walks in the door a half hour or so later, Babe and I each kinda look him over while pretending we aren't at all concerned.

And when he offers me a ride back to my room after chatting a bit about what jobs we have before us later today, I say, "No thanks, Red. I think I'll walk."

The stores along Main Street are about to open their doors. I decide it's time to dress for the Arctic if I am going to be able to keep up with Warden Hooper.

I walk to the Johnson Woolen Mills and buy myself some long underwear, a couple pairs of heavy socks and mittens.

And then, I go walk down the street, climb the stairs, unlock the door and collapse in bed.

From that day forward, I carried about every type of cold weather protection I could when working with Red. It was clear the old man had some special antifreeze in his blood.

And for the rest of my tour of duty with him, I bit my tongue and never again suggested it might be time to leave a stake out—no matter how cold, tired or hungry I might be.

I wasn't so much concerned about Red's ability to take care of business or even the fear of losing my job.

I just didn't want to have Babe glaring at me across a table like that again.

"I jumped back like I'd just found a shrunken head. I straightened up so fast I banged the back of my head on the Impala's trunk latch."

Rememberin' Red
Pesky Paychecks

Contributed by Richard Hislop

When I rode with Red, his cruiser was a Chevy Impala.

These were low riding massive metal monsters—they didn't make 'em much bigger. Lean down into the trunk of a new one and shout and you might just hear an echo.

And despite driving one of the bigger cars on the road, Red was still able to chock his car to the gills with stuff.

I was forever having to sweep away coats and files and binoculars and gun cases and boots and paper to make enough room to sit down beside him when he would pick me up. Of course, part of his storage issue was Smokey—who took up most of the back seat.

It was one of those situations where you pretend it's no big deal having to hoe out a place to sit down, and just hope you don't break anything—or worse—stab yourself in the behind with a fish hook, knife, gun barrel or who knows what.

215

Red would mumble an apology and act like he was going to take care of it before we got together the next time.

But after a couple days of this, I realized his apology was more of a ritual—a kind of welcoming ceremony—than an action plan.

But while he might not care about housekeeping, making certain the Impala ran well was important to him. And with a trainee on duty, he decided one day I was just the fellow to drive the cruiser on down into Johnson and wait while the shop tuned her up.

"Fred'll take care of you," he said, and he told me how to get there.

I said okay and climbed behind the steering wheel and headed down the road.

I rolled into the yard of a nondescript two bay gas station auto repair shop with the usual collection of junks alongside, a stack of old tires and rusted parts sitting outside.

I parked off to the side of the bays and walked into the office.

Before I could even open my mouth, the man behind the counter said, "That Hooper's cruiser?"

I nodded.

"You're not bringing that in here until all the dynamite is out of the trunk," the fellow said in no uncertain terms.

I was stunned.

"There's no dynamite in the trunk," I replied.

The fellow looked at me like I had just fallen off the Bumpkin Bus, sighed and shook his head.

"Oh, yes, there IS," he said looking hard in my eyes. "And that rig is not coming into my shop until the dynamite is outta that trunk."

Well, the only way to prove the fellow wrong was to go search the trunk.

No need to argue about it.

"Okay, I'll go look," I shrugged.

I turned around and walked back to the cruiser, found the key to the trunk, popped the lid and found it stuffed with enough gear to launch an expedition to the Sahara and the Arctic—both.

Snowshoes, waders, casting reels, fly rods, dog leashes, canvas tarps, cardboard boxes full of car parts, sugaring buckets full of various sizes and styles of taps, hammers, screwdrivers, wrenches, pieces of plywood, a good stack of 2 x 4 x almost 4s, coffee cans filled with nails and screws.

He's got a tool shed on wheels.

I tugged and shifted all this stuff around while muttering to myself what in the world my boss was doing carrying all this stuff around in the cruiser.

I mean, he could have left some of it at home, you know?

I was convinced I was just going through the motions to humor the shop owner who must only like to work on uncluttered cars.

That's when I yanked a dirty cloth off the top of an old wooden fruit box way up over the wheel well and there it was—a nice neat stack of a dozen or more sticks of dynamite—lying there together like they were nothing more than sardines in a can.

I jumped back like I'd just found a shrunken head. I straightened up so fast I banged the back of my head on the inside of the Impala's trunk latch.

"Holy Mother of God!" I shouted out in prayer.

I thought of all the miles I'd ridden with the boss, dropping, slamming and dragging the back end of the cruiser over boulders and ledge. Dynamite is set off by concussive force.

It wouldn't take but a bad slam on a logging road or a rear end collision at a stoplight for Red and me to be blown to Kingdom Come.

As I stand there rubbing the back of my head, I look up and see the garage owner standing just inside an empty bay door wiping the grease from his hands on a rag and smiling.

He'd been watching me to make certain I did a thorough search.

He shouts over, "Find 'em?" and laughs.

It was clear from the way I jumped back and the shocked look on my face that I'd come across something that had scared me.

I developed an instant case of laryngitis.

I just nodded.

"Take it all outta there and put it way over there near the barrel," the owner ordered.

I looked at him, still stunned, but starting to come to a bit. My mind was catching up with what my eyes had just seen.

I'm thinking, "No wonder Red drives so slow. Maybe it isn't just him getting up in age a bit. Maybe he's just always taking into consideration the big bomb in the trunk he carries with us everywhere we go. I guess that's a good thing..."

Well, I still had to move it.

I looked over and saw a trash barrel to my left and plotted out a path to it in my head, like a man walking through a minefield. I bent down and very gently wriggled the wooden box out of its wedged position between rubber boots, a car jack and a mess of rusty tools.

I took a deep breath and lifted the box up as carefully as a three tiered wedding cake and carried it over and set it on the ground.

I heard the garage phone ring and was some relieved when my witness turned and trotted inside the building to answer it. This guy was enjoying the look of terror on my face way too much.

I stood there just staring at the nest of perfectly placed red sticks for a bit—all sandwiched together as neat as a package of pencils—then shook my head. I walked back to the trunk and shut it up, breathed deep, plastered a big fake smile on my face and headed on inside the repair shop to announce, "Mission accomplished."

The mechanic had just hung up the phone and was leaning on one elbow and scribbling a phone number on a greasy pad of paper with a curled left arm.

"Dynamite's out of the trunk. Should be good to go," I said cheerily. I put hanging around a car repair shop just a step above a visit to the dentist on my Fun Things To Do List.

The owner stopped writing in his appointment book, cocked his head up towards me like a crow and asked, "What about the blasting caps?"

"Blasting caps?" I repeat.

"A-yuh! They're in there somewhere and you gotta find 'em and get those outta there too before that rig rolls into my shop."

I thought to myself, "How come Fred knows what Red has in here and I know nothing?"

I stood there considering the new daunting task in front of me—searching inside the cruiser crammed with all manner of gear for a tiny box of blasting caps.

I could be here for another hour tearing the cruiser apart.

I guess the look on my face sorta said it all.

Fred takes pity on me.

As much fun as he might have had watching me tear apart the entire car like some Border Patrol agent, I suppose he also wanted to just do the tune up and move on to other customers.

"Try the glove box," he said with a knowing smile just before his phone rang again.

"Okay," I nodded.

Then, I thought, "Wait a minute! The glove box —as in the one right next to the radio?"

When you drive past open quarries, there are often big signs posted telling people they must turn off their radios.

The reason is the signals have been known to set off blasting caps, and if a worker was setting a dynamite charge when you were listening to your favorite tunes or changing the stations—well, you get the picture—and it's not pretty.

So, one of the last places you would want to keep your blasting caps is in the glove box.

I walked back to the cruiser, opened the passenger door, pushed the mound of stuff on over to the driver's side, sat down and popped open the glove box.

It too was crammed with stuff: pencil stubs, leaky pens, receipts of all kinds, cruiser registrations dating back five or more years, an assortment of screws and nails, car fuses, a couple ancient candy bars, pieces of dog biscuits and finally a dirty, crumpled fist sized cardboard box with a faded "DANGER" warning on top.

I lifted it gingerly, set it down on the dash and opened it—and there they were—a couple dozen blasting caps staring back at me like perch eyes.

I saw my life flash before my eyes. I realized
I'd been patrolling the back roads sitting on top
of a bomb.

Oh my.

I slid out of the cruiser with the box of
detonators in my hands—holding the box out in
front of me like it's a treasure—and head over to
show Fred.

But once again he's a step ahead of me. He saw
me coming and shouts out, "Found 'em?"

I nod and hold out the box with a sheepish grin
on my face.

"Well, don't bring 'em in here!" he shouted at
me, stopping me in my tracks. "Put 'em out
there somewhere in the yard, FAR AWAY from
the dynamite!"

Good advice. I spun on my heel and headed
off in the opposite direction and set them
down as gently as a butterfly on a tiny corner
of lawn as far from the dynamite sticks as
I could get.

And now the fellow has me thinking, "What else
is in Red's car? What else is in there that might
kill us?"

I decided to do Red a favor and clean and
organize his cruiser while I'm here. Maybe I'm
doing myself a favor, too.

"I might as well clean the cruiser out before I bring it in," I yell to Fred.

"That'd be good!" he bellers back and for the first time he actually smiles. "Use the trash barrels. Be my guest."

I rolled a couple of the barrels up close to the Impala and dug in. There's tons of old newspapers, clothes and boots and boxes of shells. I make piles of the stuff I intend to put back inside and start tossing the paper into the trash barrels.

Just about everything in the cruiser bore the Smokey seal of approval—paw prints and black or silver dog hair.

I made one pile for receipts, another for clothes, another for guns and ammo and kept tossing the paper.

As I dug down, I kept coming across sealed blue envelopes—which is what the state used at the time to issue paychecks. I had no idea why my boss was hoarding blue envelopes, but I knew he'd get more of them soon, so into the trash they went.

The dirt and dog hair was flying from my frenetic flurry when about five minutes later a little voice inside my head told me maybe I should take a closer look at those couple of dozen blue envelopes I had just tossed into a burn barrel.

I backed outta the cruiser, straightened up and sauntered over to the tub and pawed around until I saw a blue corner. I pick it out of the trash and hold the envelope up to the sun, to let the light shine through.

Looks like there's paper in there. A paycheck, maybe?

I shake my head and dig around in the trash and pull out another one and hold it up to the light.

Same result. There's something inside there. I look hard at the envelope flaps. Looks like they've never been opened.

I can't believe it. Here I am struggling to save every penny and my boss appears to have paychecks he doesn't even bother to cash?

Is this for real?

I wasn't jealous. I was in awe. I start rummaging back through the trash grabbing up every crumpled, stained blue envelope I can find.

I laid them one by one on the dash and hold them down with a couple boxes of shells.

By the time I'm done, there's 26 unopened blue envelopes stacked in three piles.

Toss them or save them?

I decided I'd better hold onto them just in case I was right.

After almost two hours of cleaning the cruiser, it finally got into the shop for it's one hour service. The oil was changed, new plugs, points and condenser put in, along with a new distributor cap. I signed the bill and Fred backed it up out of the bay.

Now, it was time to reload the Chevy. I put the dynamite back in the trunk, covered the box up with a piece of plywood that was bigger than the box itself to keep anything from slamming into the sticks, carefully replaced the waders, fishin' poles, boots, sap buckets, taps, and shotguns, blankets, tarps, snowshoes, canteen and all of Smokey's stuff, too.

I put the blasting caps in my breast pocket and the stack of blue envelopes went inside my jacket, which I laid folded beside me on the driver's seat.

When I pulled into Red's driveway, he came out to meet me.

The cruiser looked darn near immaculate on the inside. The only thing missing was flowers on the dash.

"Been gone all morning," he noted. "Was there a problem with the car?"

"Oh, your friend, Fred, he had a few concerns

about dynamite and little things like that," I said nonchalantly. I looked to see the reaction on Red's face.

Red snorted and pushed a boot a few inches across the porch deck. "Fred worries too much," he said with a shrug.

"The good news is I did a spring cleaning on the cruiser for you—she's all spic and span inside," I said.

The dynamite issue hadn't gotten a rise out of him. But the idea that I had organized his clutter did.

Red's eyes widened and a look of concern comes over his face.

"You did?" he said.

Red stepped off the porch to take a look inside his mobile office.

"Yeah, sure was a lot of stuff in there to throw away. There was a bunch of old newspapers and worn out rags and oh yeah, a couple dozen or more of those blue envelopes—I tossed all the old paper into Fred's burn barrel for you," I said with a big smile.

Red, who had been walking around the car peering in the windows, looked a little stunned.

"You did?" Red said. I could see his mind was

racing trying to figure out how he was going
to handle this. Red wasn't the kinda fellow
to start stomping his foot and hollering at me
—especially when I was standing there wagging
my tail like a big lab puppy who had just
brought him his slippers—all chewed
to pieces.

"I sure did," I said beaming a big grin at him.

Red's eyes went up and around and his
mouth screwed up into a twisted bow. He
started shaking his head and running his
hands through his hair in frustration.
But he doesn't say a word.

He saw stacked and organized piles of
clothes, and shells and Smokey's blanket
laid out smooth and tucked into the back
bench seat.

I let him stew for a good 30 seconds or so and
then I decided to end the fun before I gave my
boss a heart attack.

"Yup, all the newspapers went in the trash.
But then I thought maybe I oughtta look a little
closer at some of your mail."

Red's head pops up from peering inside the
cruiser. He looked at me intently, listening.

"When I saw all those blue envelopes—that
didn't look like they'd even been opened—I
fished 'em all back out of the trash."

I reached inside my coat and pulled out a big, fanning pile of tattered, paw print stained blue envelopes.

"And here they are," I said handing them over to him.

Red's frown vanished. He shook his head and laughed.

"By the Judas Priest, Dick! You had me a'goin," he chuckled as he accepted the fat stack into his big hands.

He pursed his lips, shook the envelopes like they were a court summons, and said, "These are a nuisance to me."

"Red, how can that be?" I asked incredulously.

"I'll tell you why," he said. And Red proceeded to explain that the paychecks required him going to the bank, when he'd rather be out working in the woods.

And when he couldn't get to his bank on the days and hours it was open, he had to save the checks somewhere until he could go. If the envelopes landed on the dash, they fell to the floor. If he stuffed them in a coat pocket, he'd find himself wearing a different coat when he finally got to the bank.

"I'll show you just what trouble these things cause," Red said and he turned to walk back into the house and called over his shoulder to me, "Come on inside."

He walked on over to a secretary—not the human kind—but a desk style that has a writing table, pigeon holes above and drawers beneath.

There were stacks and stacks of papers lying on the writing surface in crooked piles—much of it related to his maple sugaring operation.

I waited while Red pawed through the piles muttering to himself, "I know I have it here somewhere..."

"Ah! Here 'tis," he said with a sly smile and he handed me a brief typed letter with the State of Vermont seal at the top of it.

"Read this," he said, grinning mischievously.

I looked closer and saw the letter was from the Vermont Department of Taxes.

My eyebrows shot up. Red—who never misses a twitch—grinned bigger at my reaction and said, "Go on. Read it out loud."

"Dear Mr. Hooper, The State of Vermont is unable to close its books for the previous fiscal year until you cash your paychecks," the letter said—in slightly fancier legalese, since some lawyer wrote it.

"Please, cash your paychecks immediately."

It was signed by the Commissioner of Taxes and it was dated two years earlier.

I looked up at Red—incredulous.

Red looked back at me and winked.

It was clear he loved that letter. And he wasn't about to change his ways for anybody.

Direct Deposit—where the money goes straight into your bank account?

I think that was invented just for Red.

"I feel like I'm under orders to watch the snow screen on a black and white TV and take notes."

Eyes in the Forest

Contributed by Richard Hislop

I n the first couple days of working with Red, he hikes me into the back country of Hyde Park, over near Garfield in an area called "The Diggings."

He's an impressive walker, with long legs and a knowing way in the woods.

He leads me up to a spot overlooking some beaver ponds and down below we spy a couple guys fishing.

Red motions for me to stop and I nod.

He reaches for his binoculars. We're maybe 100 yards above these fellows, hidden by some alder brush.

We watch these fellows for hours in silence—standing, sitting, crouching. Red never says a word. He raises his binoculars once in awhile to get a closer look while this fellow reels in a fish. But that's about it.

The sun comes up and over the big pines off to our left.

These guys aren't doing anything too exciting that I can see—they're bait fishing. Once in awhile they get a bite, most of the time they don't.

I'm a 25 year old guy used to moving. I want to do something. Standing around in silence is torture for me. I feel like I'm under orders to watch the snow screen on a black and white TV and take notes.

This goes on for hours. It's all I can do not to scream.

Finally, Red sighs, turns to me and whispers, "Okay," and he turns to walk back to the cruiser.

"Aren't we going to go check their creels and licenses?" I whisper back.

"No," Red says over his shoulder and he continues to walk back the way we came in about five hours earlier.

I stumble after him in silence. My mind is screaming, "Are you kidding me?"

I'm biting my tongue just about hard enough to draw blood.

I don't get it. But I'm smart enough not to offer my opinion or ask the boss any questions.

When I get to my room hours later, I am still fuming, thinking if this is the way Warden Hooper works, I'll go nuts before my tour is up. The next day, we're back on patrol and things go better. I kinda let this incident go and just hope he doesn't make me stand there for hours again.

About two weeks later, Red and I swing into a country store to pick up some supplies when a young fellow comes out the door headed to his car swinging a gallon jug of milk in one hand and a loaf of bread in the other.

"Hello, Mike," Red says all warden friendly. The guy looks a little surprised but says hello back to Red, who has stopped to have a conversation with him.

"Nice mess of Brookies you and Sean caught over at the Diggins the other day," Red says to him.

The guy's back stiffens like someone had just grabbed him by the back of the neck and given him a shake. He about dropped the milk.

"You, you were there?" he stammers in shock. And then I recognize him—he's one of the fellows who was fishing in the backcountry about two weeks ago.

The youngster has a look on his face like his mom just caught him looking a little too long at a picture of an underwear model in one of her glossy magazines.

"Sure," Red says. "You got some nice fish," and Red proceeds to tell the young man exactly what he reeled in and Sean, too, all from memory.

Then Red changes the subject to say something nice about the young man's parents and ask about how his big brother, Tom, is liking Army life.

The kid mumbles, "He likes it okay, I guess."

But I can see from his shifty eyes and weak smile, he's in shock thinking about how Red had been watching him all that time he was fishing in the back country and the kid never had a clue.

And right then, I get it.

If we'd marched on down the hill and asked to see Mike and Sean's fishing licenses and checked their creels, we might have found a violation, maybe not.

But now we had a fellow who was on notice there could be a warden watching him no matter how deep he hiked into the backcountry with his fishing pole—or shotgun, bow or deer rifle for that matter.

Red said, "Well, I don't want that jug of milk to sour on you," adding, "Say hello to your parents for me," and walked on into the store.

I followed after Red, but slowly, and kept one eye on the boy.

236

I saw him trip over a crack in the sidewalk and looking back over his shoulder a time or two at Red in disbelief.

I smiled.

This young man will be sharing his brief encounter with Red within minutes—casting a line, handing a buddy a wrench or hoisting a beer. My bet is he'll be telling the story for years to come.

I can hear him as plain as day saying, "Just 'cause you don't see him, don't mean Hooper or some other warden ain't around watchin' your every move. You do what you want. I'm just warnin' you is all."

Patience pays.

It was a valuable lesson and one I used time and again over the course of my own career.

"I see Smokey trying to eat the window glass and snarling and barking and squealing—he wants so bad to get at the mini mutt on the snow below."

Rememberin' Red
Boy Scout Manners

CONTRIBUTED BY RICHARD HISLOP

Have you ever noticed that some of the meanest people in the world have the friendliest dogs and the nicest folks have some of the meanest mutts?

I kinda think the ankle biting, pants ripping canines figure their owners are nasty enough for the two of them, so the dogs can just kick back and relax.

And that the mean dogs figure if their owner is going to be such a trusting sap, the pooch had better step up, take charge and be a vicious son of a gun to protect the house 'cause Mister Too Trusting sure ain't gonna get the job done.

It's just a theory. Someone should interview the dogs, I guess.

Anyhow, Red had one of the biggest, most intimidating, not to be messed with German Shepherds you would ever not want to meet—Smokey.

Smokey was one of a long line of German Shepherds Red used as a furry deputy. He called them all Smokey. I think this one was number six or seven—something like that.

This particular Smokey protected Red and the cruiser as if he was a mama crocodile with a nest full of eggs. Come within 15 feet of the man or the cruiser and be prepared to go home with dirty shorts, serious blood loss—or both.

Even Red had his hands full with his big bad wolf.

Red kept a stick in the front seat with him and when Smokey got to barking and slobbering so much even Red couldn't stop him or stand it, Red would wave that stick over his right shoulder and shout at Smokey "BE QUIET," like a lion tamer. He never hit the dog. It was just to get his attention is all.

Red loved the dog and most of the time spoke to him as if he was a child.

But for those of us who weren't all that familiar to Smokey, it was a little scary to be around the Shepherd, because the dog didn't listen to anyone but Red, and there were times Smokey was pretty selective in his hearing even then.

This was a concern for trainees who needed to ride with Red and would have appreciated not having to worry about having our throats ripped out when getting into the cruiser or reaching for something in the back seat.

Red made it clear when I signed on with him that I should NEVER EVER just open a cruiser door and climb inside unless Red climbed in first and told Smokey he should leave me alone.

"Careful! He nips," Red advised.

Smokey was 100 plus pounds of fighting trim and gleaming white wolf teeth. I couldn't imagine the beast nipping. I could imagine him tearing an arm off and relishing every shake.

Red's devotion to his shark in a dog suit was exceptional, too. He made certain the dog was comfortable and well fed.

Red was trim, never a fellow who looked like he fought the scale like some of us. And I swear a calculated part of his staying fit was the fact he gave a good half of his lunch every day to Smokey—who, like most dogs, never met a meal he didn't like.

Still, the man dog partnership was a smart move for an aging warden working alone.

The dog made young bucks with something to hide, think twice about running away or giving him any lip.

Smokey scared the hell out of most everyone

just by sitting quietly next to his boss and staring into your eyes.

You always had the sense that with just one word from Red, Smokey would have you on the ground and his jaws around your neck in about two seconds.

More than once I saw Red talk to some fellows who were a little reluctant to cooperate.

Smokey sensed the tension in the air and stood up slowly, the hair between his shoulders rising. The dog took one step forward, looked each of them in the eyes and licked his chops—just once.

Believe me, a dog like Smokey instantly turns the most belligerent suspect into an altar boy.

Red did a lot of fellows a big favor when he'd say, "Smokey, sit!"

Which reminds me of a story of Roy Hood, another veteran warden I trained with down in southern Vermont. Like Red, Roy was getting close to retirement when I worked with him, too.

And, like Red, Roy had a German Shepherd travel with him while on patrol. Roy named his deputy dog, "Abbott."

But compared to Smokey, Abbott was a pussycat. You could actually tag along with Roy

and Abbott and not feel like you were bothering
a badger with a sore tooth.

Still, it was clear Abbott also had the
breeding to step up and protect his boss in
a pinch.

One day Roy, Abbott and I are out on patrol
checking fishing licenses along a branch of the
Black River when we came across a couple of
fellows attempting to fill their creels.

We walk down to the stream bank and greet
them.

We have a polite introduction and brief
conversation. The fellows are cooperative and
produce their fishing licenses and show me
their catch.

As we chat with them, Abbott sits just beside
Roy, who is watching me do the license and
creel checks. I'm in training after all.

I can see one of the guys shifting from foot
to foot and keeping a close eye on Abbott.
He's uncomfortable being this close to that
big dog.

I can't say I blame him. It can be pretty
intimidating if you aren't familiar with dogs.

Everything checks out with the fishermen.
After a bit more small talk, Roy and I wish
them a nice day and good luck fishing.

As Roy and I turn to leave, the twitchy fellow asks, "Say warden, why do you bring that big dog along with you?"

Roy, who is married to an exceptionally good cook, Jennie, and has the girth to prove it, responds in his high voiced lisp, "Welth, Fellawths, ith like thith."

He pauses, straightens up to his full height and sucks in a deep breath. That allows him to pooch out his belly to its full glory above his shiny black gun belt.

Roy traces his gut with both hands like a proud expectant mother in her eighth month of pregnancy, and grins at them.

"You see, I can't wun like I youthta," he explains with an exaggerated sad pout—his lower lip reminds me of Shirley Temple in one of her old movies.

Then he turns his gaze to Abbott, who is sitting in between Roy and me and gazing back up at Roy, just itching for a command. "But HE can," Roy grins and winks.

"Oh," says the nervous fellow, his eyes showing more than a little fear. I watch as both of these guys stiffen their backs like frozen perch on January ice.

"Come on, Abbott," Roy says, turning to walk away from the men. Abbott turns to follow Roy and I tag along behind, trying not to bust out laughing.

Roy was absolutely right. An obedient deputy dog really helps.

But Smokey wasn't as good natured as Abbott.

You just never knew what was going to set the dog off into his over the top I'm gonna eat you alive attack mode.

Take the time Red stopped by the Post Office in downtown Johnson with Smokey and me in the car on a clear, frosty January morning.

I knew Red would be awhile. Everyone knew him and whenever he showed up anywhere, folks wanted to chat with him and he was generally happy to oblige.

Like any warden, you get a lot of tips that way.

So, knowing the boss would be a good half hour or more just dropping off a letter and buying a few stamps, I decided to stretch my legs.

I get out of the cruiser and am standing on the sidewalk a foot or two outside the passenger door just enjoying the sun on my face and looking around.

Smokey was sleeping in the back seat when we pulled up. As ever, Red had the back windows down a hefty third of the way so the dog could get fresh air and not be steaming up the windows.

All was well until this older woman comes down the sidewalk walking a tiny white toy poodle. She's a large woman dressed up in a dark blue wool coat with a faux fur collar, gloves and black boots with a small heel—a hand bag over one arm and a red leash holding back the tiny dog in the other.

I smile and look at the dog—which is like a kid's toy with brand new batteries. He is skittering across the ice and snow on his tiny legs and straining at the end of his six foot tether—moving back and forth across the sidewalk like a vacuum cleaner sucking up invisible loose change.

His little legs are moving so fast they're a blur.

I make sure my size 12 boots are firmly planted on the sidewalk as the dog passes me so there is no chance I might squish the thing like an ant by accident.

As the matron crosses the car's grill, I smile and lift my hand to tip my Smokey Bear hat to her. I'm on the "g" in "Good Morning," when all hell breaks loose just behind me.

Smokey.

I don't know whether Smokey smelled the tiny canine or heard it's paws skittering on the snow or just got bored and decided to have a little fun and shake the hell out of downtown Johnson and me.

He couldn't possibly have considered this toy dog and its owner a threat, could he?

Maybe he was thinking "snack."

Anyhow, Smokey jumps up, sticks his head out the window and lets loose a series of insane attack barks and snarls whose decibel level could only be matched by Civil War cannon fire.

I jump about three feet off the ground, twist in the air and land facing the back door in a crouch. I'm ready for any and everything.

I see Smokey trying to eat the window glass and snarling and barking and squealing—he wants so bad to get at the mini mutt on the snow below.

He's insane.

Smokey is so worked up he's sending big long gobs of dog spit flying out onto the sidewalk and drool is oozing down both sides of the window glass.

The poor poodle has no idea what is happening. But for sure, it must see its life flash before its eyes.

The tiny mutt launches like a sled dog to the

end of its six foot leash and is stopped dead by
the shiny rhinestone collar. The dog's mouth
opens in a pant as it tries to pull away. But
there's no way the six pound poodle is going to
budge his 200 plus pound owner, who is stopped
dead and trying to turn away from the monster.

The lady is as shocked as I am.

She looks up at me like I am playing some sort
of cruel practical joke on her.

I can't blame her.

One second, I'm a friendly officer of the law
greeting her with a big smile and making her feel
oh so special and a split second later I appear to
have loosed a hound from hell on her.

I turn and yell to Smokey, "STOP!"

I might as well have shouted at the parking
meter. He pays absolutely no attention to me.

The mutt knows he outranks me.

I look down and see the poodle is straining on
his lead and collar, spinning its paws on the
snow and ice—like a miniature 18 wheeler losing
traction on an icy hill despite chains.

The tiny dog is on his hind feet and pulling for
all its worth. No way is this mini mutt going
to tow this massive matriarch along the snow
slicked sidewalk like a sled dog.

Realizing he can't move forward, and tired of choking himself to death, the poodle turns counterclockwise and bolts.

My mouth falls open as I see him wrap his lead tight around the lady's ankles—like a champion calf roper at the national rodeo finals.

He's a blur.

He might have set a new world record for ankle roping.

Of course, the blue haired matron wants to run from the scene to save herself and her pet. She tries taking a step back.

But with her ankles roped, that's a big no go.

She's unable to see what is going on below her ample bosom. I say, "Hold still, Ma'am!" But Smokey's barking and snarling makes it impossible for her to hear me.

She looks up at me and her mouth makes a little "o" like she's asking me what in the world is happening.

Her head wobbles like a bobble head toy. Her shoulders shudder and then the faux fur collar of her coat jumps like the mink is coming back to life.

A look of terror comes into her eyes. She realizes she's about to topple over like a fir in the forest. Only this is downtown Johnson and there's ice and cement beneath us.

I'm thinking, "If she falls and bangs her head on the curb or the cruiser or both, Red and Smokey and I are all in a world of trouble. I gotta do something here."

I turn my attention from Smokey and step in behind the lady to make the save.

It's like I'm trying to catch a bushel basket of Peaslee's Potatoes with a catcher's mitt.

I mean, there's a lot of lady here and my hands are only so big.

I stand behind her and throw one arm around her ample waist like we're getting ready to tango and step in close.

If she crumps, I'm hoping my knees will catch her ample derriere and break her fall before she hits the sidewalk. At least it will be a gentle landing.

She falls back away from the cruiser and into my arms. Her boot toes are sticking up in the air like the witch in the Wizard of Oz movie.

I tow her back the way she came—a good 10 feet away from the cruiser's grill—in hopes of getting Smokey to calm down and shut up.

The poodle is lying on his side with his pink

tongue out dragging along with us and panting. He's done in.

My backing up and towing the lady and her tiny dog away from the cruiser finally gets Smokey to stop barking.

I guess he figures he's done his job and he's proud of himself for chasing this desperado away so's I could
arrest her.

Or maybe he is just pausing for a second and searching for a throat lozenge so he can start up again. I don't know.

I exhale, then breathe deep and boost the lady back onto her feet planting my size 12s solidly on the snow. I push up with my shoulders and elbows and stifle a groan.

Once she's on her feet, it's time for me to try and revive her dog.

I steady her with one arm, get down on one knee and say, "Please, hold still just a second, Ma'am, and I'll get you untangled."

The poodle is prostrate and panting.

I pick him up with one hand and unwind him and the lead together—he doesn't put up any kind of a fight.

The dog is so small—it feels like a Popsicle stick

someone glued cotton balls onto. His heart is beating as fast as a hummingbird's.

I hand the dog up to her and she begins cooing.

The poodle's cotton tail starts beating and the dog gives her cheek a big lick. Well, big by his standards. In actuality, the dog's tongue is the size of a pencil eraser.

I get back on my feet, take a deep breath and try again to give her my best nice introductory smile. I'm hoping maybe we can start over.

I start apologizing. Profusely.

Which is pretty crazy if you think about it.

I am begging her to forgive this nutty dog that isn't mine, a dog that would just as soon bite me as look at me, a dog that I wished more than once would just have a heart attack and keel over dead—and then felt awful about even thinking that, because he's the old man's dog and best friend.

Lucky for Red and Smokey and me, this lady is softhearted.

Once she sees her pooch is okay, she thanks me for my help.

But there's still the issue of getting her past Smokey.

I offer to escort her across the street, away from the cruiser with the crazed canine, and she accepts.

Red comes out of the Post Office a few minutes later—just in time to see me walking the matron across the street.

She's holding onto my arm and her poodle is skittering ahead in the snow like the world's smallest reindeer.

When I return to the cruiser, Red looks at me, smiles and says, "That was awful nice of you."

I bite my tongue, smile and nod.

I don't say a word.

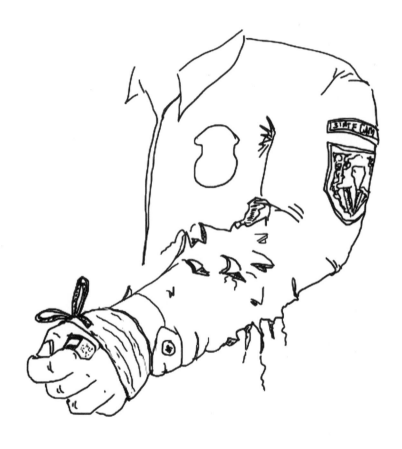

"Smokey's fangs are glistening pearly white from frothy doggie drool and he's snapping his jaws like a barracuda. He's ready to tear into anything."

REMEMBERIN' RED
HITCHHIKER

CONTRIBUTED BY ERIC NUSE

C ompared to a ride I shared with Red and Smokey, I think maybe Hislop got off easy that wintry day in Johnson.

It was summer. Red was driving along Route 15 through Craftsbury, with me on the bench seat beside him and Smokey asleep in the back.

Red sees a young man with his thumb out, hitchhiking, and for whatever reason, the boss decides to pull over and give the kid a lift.

I'm thinking, "Has Red lost his mind? Smokey is not going to like this!"

When the cruiser slows and its tires hit the gravel shoulder of the road, the dog knows something is up.

Smokey rouses himself, sits up on his haunches, yawns and takes a look around.

The dog spies the young man running towards the Cruiser—a smile on his face and his backpack swinging in his hand.

255

The kid's happy to be getting a ride. Who knows how long he's been standing there?

This isn't exactly a high traffic area.

Smokey interrupts this happy hitchhiker scene by launching into his "We're being attacked!" bark.

The kid keeps coming at the car.

He must hear the dog barking, but what hitchhiker would think a driver—especially an officer of the law—would pull over just to let his dog tear him to pieces, right?

I see disaster ahead.

If that boy opens the car door and jumps in the backseat, Red's next stop will be a hospital emergency room—or worse—a morgue.

Smokey clearly thinks the young man is a threat and intends to tear him apart.

I can't believe Red thinks this is going to go well.

With each trotting step the young man makes towards the cruiser, Smokey goes more insane.

Spit tossing, drool flinging, ear deafening outta control roars and clawing at the glass, trying to eat the upholstery, rabid dog insanity.

I turn and look at Red. Even though he's just a
foot from me, I can't hear a word he's saying.

But I can see him mouthing the words,
"Be Quiet!" and "Calm down!" to Smokey.

The only sound in the cruiser is relentless,
deafening "BARK!BARK!BARK!BARK!" from the
dog, right in my ear.

Well, somebody has got to do something, and
fast.

So, I open the passenger seat door just wide
enough for me to slide out.

I slam the door shut before Smokey leaps into
the front seat and follows me.

Then I run to the hitchhiker and intercept him
12 feet from the cruiser.

He can't hear me because of the dog's barking.

But, I motion to him to take the seat up front,
beside Red, where I was just sitting.

The kid nods. He's still smiling, but his eyes
show concern.

Then I take off my jacket, wrap it around my
left forearm and jump into the back seat, beside
the insanely barking, thrashing Smokey.

Smokey's fangs are glistening pearly white

with frothy doggie drool and he's snapping his jaws up and down like a barracuda.

He's a coiled spring that is wound so tight, it's got to snap.

I reach my left arm in front of the dog's gaping jaws as the young man opens the passenger door to climb in.

The kid has a smile on his face, but he's looking over his left shoulder with fear in his eyes.

He's wondering about this crazed German Shepherd.

Is this dog undercontrol?

Red is still shouting at Smokey to calm down, his face is flushed with anger and frustration.

Smokey lunges as the young man slides onto the bench seat next to Red, leans forward and drops his backpack on the car floor between his feet.

My arm is there.

Smokey slams his jaws onto my forearm like a shark on a mackerel.

He's so wound up, he does the neck twisting, doggie death thrash a few times, too.

He lifts me right out of the seat.

Why did I do it?

Well, he was going to bite someone and I figured it had better be me.

So, I'm just sayin', I kinda think Hislop was lucky to have trained with Red and Smokey during the winter months.

The hitchhikers had already thumbed their way South.

"And with the .357 he's never fired before
and the borrowed eyeglasses balanced
upside down on his nose like he's a seal
with a ball, when "Hooper!" is called,
Red proceeds to the firing line."

Rememberin' Red
HOTSHOT

CONTRIBUTED BY DENNY GAIOTTI

Once a year the wardens would get together over in Middlesex for a mandatory shooting match.

Our shooting skills were tested standing, crouching, lying down, etc.

It was serious business, but a time for a little friendly competition and camaraderie as well.

So most of us would visit a firing range in the weeks leading up to the match to practice. And if there was any question your vision might need a tune up, we'd quietly visit an optometrist before the shoot, too.

This particular year, Red rolls in late. He'd been out on a call the night before or something.

He's a little discombobulated and pawing around his vehicle for his eyeglasses and his .357 revolver.

It doesn't take long for Red to figure out he
left in such a hurry, he left his glasses and his
weapon back home in Johnson on the kitchen
counter.

What to do?

Well, there's plenty of side arms around. Of
course, they are not tuned to Red's particular
aim and stance. And that can be an issue.

But Red borrows a .357 from another warden
who has already gone through the course.

Then he asks to try on some of the other fellows'
eyeglasses. He peers through one set of glasses
and then another and another.

We all want to help him out. I offer my glasses,
too. Red tries 'em on, but my prescription doesn't
work for his eyes. He thanks me and returns
them.

After trying on five or six, he takes the pair of
eyeglasses he says work best and he turns them
upside down—so the nose pieces are sticking
up in the air and the temples—the parts that
go over your ears—they're reaching for the sky
above his famously big ears.

And with the .357 he's never fired before and the
borrowed eyeglasses balanced on his nose like
he's a seal with a ball, when "Hooper!" is called,
Red proceeds to the firing line.

I'm standing there along with the other fellows thinking, "No way is this gonna go well." I figure we're all about to be witnesses to a real disaster.

He's using a revolver he's never fired, borrowed eyeglasses teetering upside down on his nose.

Add to this, the fact that Red's left hand is below his belly button pushing in on the hernia that is always bothering him. To hold the pistol up and steady with his right hand, he has to push in his guts with the other.

And then there's just having a shaky shooting hand from being flustered.

Pick any one of these nuisances and most folks' aim will be off big time. Add 'em all together and you're talking a train wreck. I figure Red might as well be shooting at the moon.

We're all standing back kinda uncomfortably quiet trying to think of things we can say to cheer him up later. He's known for being a good shot, but he might as well be shooting this course with a blindfold on today.

So, how did Red do?

He aced the course.

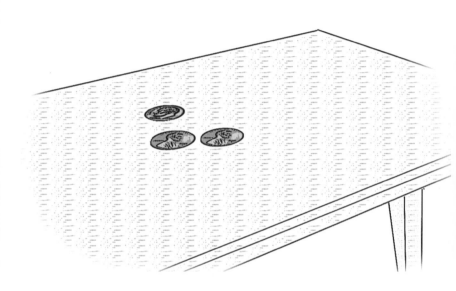

"You know, Mr. Smith, when you first came on up here and took this job, I shook my head and said to myself, 'That fella's a 10 center, for sure.' "

Rememberin' Red
Measure of a Man

CONTRIBUTED BY JOHN KAPUSTA

We had a young lawyer from down country sign on as a state prosecutor up in our service area. He was a city boy coming to give the country a try, I guess.

It wasn't long before the wardens in the area noticed he wasn't taking fish and game violations very seriously. At first we thought maybe it was just because he didn't know a bass from a blue gill. But, after some discussion with the man, we began to suspect the problem went deeper.

He didn't think it was worth his time to prosecute those accused of violating fish and game laws. The wardens in the area asked for a meeting with him. The fellow shows up in a fancy suit and spit and polish dress shoes.

He's all smiles at the front of the room while making excuse after excuse as to why he wasn't doing his job. We ask a few questions and he dodges and weaves.

He throws out all kinds of legalese to muddy

the waters further in an attempt to make us feel stupid as well. Finally, Red raises his hand. He'd been standing in the back patiently listening for about an hour, and watching.

"Yes, Warden Hooper?" the fellow says, acknowledging Red. Red stands taller and looks the fellow straight in the eye. "You know, Mr. Smith, when you first came on up here and took this job, I shook my head and said to myself, 'That fella's a 10 center, for sure.'" Some of us gulped. That's an insult—just in case you missed it.

Red pauses, purses his lips, shakes his head and then continues. We're all kinda frozen in the moment—waiting to hear what the veteran will say next. The lawyer stands there smiling and nodding, following Red's every word.

"But I see now, I was wrong about you," Red says. He takes a deep breath. His chin comes up an inch or two, his chest puffs out. A big smile comes over the prosecutor's face.

"I aimed nine cents high," Red proclaims, shaking his head in disgust. Oh my. Watching that fellow's face up at the front of the room, it was like seeing a half baked cake come outta the oven and collapse.

Mr. Excuse's shoulders sagged a good three inches and his politician's smile disappeared. Red picked up his hat and headed for the door. Well, what was there left to say? Like the chief at a tribal council of another age, the old man had spoken and there was nothing any of us could add. We all agreed with him.

Red had a way of saying out loud what everyone else was thinking. We picked up our Stetsons, and one by one followed Red out in silence. The empty suit was left with his long list of excuses as to why he wasn't doing the job and no one to tell 'em, too.

A few months later, this fellow who didn't know a varying hare from a cottontail, made front page news in the local paper by taking a job in a private law firm outside the state.

The write up in the paper had the usual glowing remarks from his boss about how he hadn't been with us long, but he sure made a difference and would be missed by all, but this new opportunity was just too good to pass up.

The usual blather. I read the story and laughed. I figured I knew what had really happened. Red had left that meeting and made a few phone calls to some friends of his—state legislators, maybe even the governor—and explained our frustration.

Those friends made a few calls. Together, they helped this young fellow see he was better suited to writing wills.

Red took care of the problem for us.

"According to this here letter, it looks like a used car dealer down there in Rutland is now runnin' the state of Vermont."

WEAR AND TEAR

CONTRIBUTED BY WAYNE ROWELL

The State of Vermont decided to lease cars for wardens, instead of buying them. Someone thought it would save money.

The fellow who got the contract was a car dealer down in Rutland.

Well, of course, when you're a car dealer and you lease vehicles, you have a big concern as to their condition when they're returned. You've still got to sell that car and they need to be clean and in good shape to do that.

And wardens can be pretty tough on a vehicle. The paint was always getting scraped off from tree branches alongside back roads. The bumpers would get chewed up on rocks and from having to be winched out of potholes deep enough to swallow a pig.

And you sure didn't want to ever look underneath the chassis of a car driven by a warden after six months of use. No doubt the oil pan and gas tank would be dented like someone had taken a ballpeen hammer to it.

But that wasn't what concerned this particular car contractor. Nope, he wanted to make certain the interiors of his leased vehicles came back in pristine condition.

That was another tall order. Many of us just about lived in our vehicles and that meant lots of coffee spills, squished jelly donuts, countless crumbs, the occasional upended tomato sauce rich pasta dish and a trunk painted with hair and blood samples from endless furred critters we removed from the woods or roadways.

But for all of those very real concerns, the memo that came through the channels to all of us was the issue of dogs riding in our vehicles.

Dogs were about to be banned from riding in the new leased cruisers.

Well, the howl of protest that went up could be heard from Pownal to Peacham.

What was a warden without his dog?

Roy Hood had his German Shepherd, Abbott. I had my Chesapeake Bay Retriever, Rover, and up north, Red Hooper had Smokey. There were young fellows coming up the ranks who might want a dog riding with them, too.

The memo might as well have said we could no longer go out on patrol wearing pants.

My supervisor called me to ask if I would be willing to pay a deposit on my cruiser, so that when it came to turn the vehicle back into the car dealership, if there was damage from Rover, I'd be paying for it.

Well, I had a wife and four children to support. My wife was working at the Wilmington Post Office and on my free days I assisted a local plumber to make extra money. But having Rover accompany me daily was so important to me, that I said, yes, I would be willing to pay a deposit.

Short of a ban on dogs in wardens' cruisers, that was one of the possible solutions on the table, when a meeting was called to discuss this issue.

Edward Kehoe was commissioner at the time.

They named the conservation camp in Castleton, overlooking the southern part of Lake Bomoseen and Birdseye Mountain after him.

Most of us thought Ed did a pretty good job.

He worked with some pretty opinionated characters—not just among the public or in the Vermont Legislature—but in his own Department.

Like Red Hooper.

Ed was in the room when Red had his say regarding the issue of dogs in leased vehicles and the doggie deposit.

Folks like to say redheads are hotheads who tend to get riled up easy and blow like a tea kettle.

And that might be true of some, but it wasn't true of Red. He had the determination they talk about redheads having, and he had courage and the guts to speak up, but he was too smart to blow his top.

Red had brought a copy of the dog deposit memo with him to the meeting. When it was time for comments he stood up and held the letter up high so's everyone could see it.

"According to this here letter, it looks like a used car dealer down there in Rutland is now runnin' the State of Vermont," Red proclaimed.

He was exaggerating, of course. But he wasn't far off the mark, if you thought about it. Banning dogs from our vehicles was a big policy change—one that could get a warden hurt or maybe even killed—all because a car dealer needed to make certain his cars came back with an interior clean enough to sell the cars to someone else.

But Red wasn't done yet.

He had words to say about the notion of a dog deposit as well.

"I challenge anyone to take a look at the back seat of my car where Smokey sits," he said, looking around the room for anyone who might want to take him up on his offer. "And then you go take a look at the front seat, where I sit."

He took another one of his dramatic pauses.

We sat spellbound.

"You won't see any difference," Red declared.

"My arse wears just as big a hole in the front seat, as my dog's does in the back."

And he nodded and stood waiting for the crowd's response.

Well, I burst out laughing as did most everyone there. And from us dog owners, Red got a hearty round of applause to boot.

Commissioner Kehoe didn't say anything.

But a week or so later we got another memo: our dogs could stay. The deposit idea was dropped, too.

And as soon as the lease expired, the State of Vermont went back to buying vehicles for us.

"By the time Red swung into the hospital parking lot some 30 plus minutes later, there was a crowd of nurses and doctors gathered to meet him outside the Emergency Room door where the ambulances pull up."

SHOT FIRED

Contributed by Richard Hislop

Whether Smokey was just wound a little too tight or so devoted to Red that he viewed everyone as a threat or what all, I don't know.

But the dog was a serious liability on this particular day following an accident that could have cost Red his life.

Red didn't much say a whole lot about it and the incident occurred some years after I trained with him.

And while some of the details are a little fuzzy after pretty near close to 50 years have passed, I'm going to tell it to you the way I heard it.

Red had a habit of jamming the muzzle of his .22 caliber Colt Woodsman pistol down the front of his pants, just above and a little in front of his right hip.

Maybe he found holsters a nuisance. But more likely Red didn't have the money to buy a holster

275

when he was a kid out hunting to put meat on the table and this is just the way he got used to carrying his sidearm—as a front arm.

When he signed on as a warden in 1935, the habit came with him and it stuck. He carried the Colt with him for many, many years without incident.

It sure wasn't regulation.

But Red had a tendency to just do things his way, so a rule wouldn't do much to stop him.

To be clear, Red didn't ride around with his Colt Woodsman revolver stuffed into his trousers. The .22 rode on the seat beside him.

Whenever he stepped out of the cruiser, he'd pick it up and tuck it in his waistband before heading out into the woods or before approaching a vehicle or a suspect.

Now, sticking a gun barrel down your pants is largely frowned upon by safety experts for a number of pretty good reasons.

Chief among them is the fact you can shoot yourself.

Secondarily, you can get the gun caught in your shirt or catch the trigger on a belt loop and slow yourself down.

Then again, the pistol can slide around and

maybe go off and shoot someone else.

And of course, even if the gun doesn't fire,
you can get hung up and caught when moving
fast through trees or crossing a stone wall or
have the weapon slip and slide right down your
pant leg into your boot—slowing you down and
maybe tripping you up.

Red knew all this.

The Woodsman had a safety switch on it,
and I am confident Red was meticulous about
sliding that little button to the safety position
before stuffing the pistol into his trousers.

But this particular day something went wrong.

Very wrong.

It happened while Red and Smokey were on
patrol together in Eden.

Red just stepped outside of the cruiser, reached
for his pistol and had just stuffed it into his
waistband, closed the door and walked off when
there was a pop like a firecracker and a sudden
stinging pain in his left leg.

Whether his bunched up shirt caught the safety
and then the trigger or his underwear or what
all happened, we'll never know.

Because Red said he never really knew himself
how it happened.

The Woodsman .22 discharged a single shot of lead into his left thigh. The bullet came out just above his knee.
Two holes.

I don't care who you are, you know, that's gotta hurt.

Red was alone—except for Smokey, of course. And being a proud Yankee of the old school, and mightily embarrassed to boot, he didn't want to put anyone out by calling and asking for help.

He managed to hobble back into the cruiser, open the driver's door and slide his behind back in front of the steering wheel.

He got his left leg propped up pretty good— elevated some on the floor mat where a pool of blood was collecting.

His right leg being operable, he could handle the cruiser's accelerator and brake pedals okay.

So, despite the searing pain and a goodly flow of blood running down his leg, into his boot and onto the cruiser's floor mat, Red took the self sufficient route like any good Yankee would.

Red called into the Lamoille County Dispatcher to report there'd been a shot fired.

When the Dispatcher asked if anyone was hurt, he told her yes—he was.

But he would be driving himself to the hospital in Morrisville—about 15 miles away. Asked if anyone else was involved, she was told "Negative."

That was all the Dispatcher needed to know to understand this was a self inflicted wound, along with everyone else with a police scanner.

In those days, most all conversations between a Dispatcher and law enforcement was broadcast over radio easily accessible to the general public.

Owning a police scanner was popular free entertainment for the public.

Some nights it seemed everybody in the Kingdom was tuned in.

Red was among the most colorful of the law enforcement officers communicating nightly from his cruiser.

He never really got into the police jargon used to summarize a situation.

His approach was more like that of a play by play radio announcer calling a Red Sox game.

If he was in the cruiser following someone, he'd relay something like this, "Well, it looks like he's stopping now. A-yup. I guess I'll stick with him and see where he goes."

For fans of "Red Radio," listening to his nightly

play by play was better than any ball game.

There'd be a pause until the other car started up again.

"Oh, he just signaled to turn right. Smokey and I will just see what he does next."

Of course, this was one time the Dispatcher wanted Red to keep talking. There was concern he would black out before he ever got himself to the hospital.

The Dispatcher offered to send an ambulance, state police and the like.

But Red insisted on driving himself.

"No, no," he said. "I'll be there shortly."

They lost contact with Red for a good 10 to 20 minutes.

One of the stories told about that lost period is that Red actually pulled over to let Smokey jump out and pee.

Folks who knew Red and how devoted he was to the dog, don't doubt he'd actually do that.

We do know he never turned on his siren or blue lights or sped up to get to the hospital in Morrisville.

He just drove as he always did—which is to

say—very slow, stopping at every stop sign and looking both ways.

By the time Red swung into the hospital parking lot some 30 plus minutes later, there was a crowd of nurses and doctors gathered to meet him outside the Emergency Room door where the ambulances pull up.

The dozen or so staff in blue and white and green smocks and coats were there along with a gurney and IV poles, oxygen tanks and heart jumping machines and all manner of modern life saving machinery.

Smokey took one look at these strangers— hospital gowns billowing into the breeze, strange caps on their heads, some of them even tying white masks over their faces—all rushing toward his boss's car and reaching for the door handles.

The Shepherd went ballistic beyond belief.

Maybe the dog was reminded of an unwanted visit to his vet's office in addition to what he viewed as a full out assault on his castle—the cruiser.

You remember how Smokey reacted to the poodle the size of a squirrel, right? About to eat glass to get at it.

Well then, you can begin to imagine how Smokey reacted to six or more men and women running up toward the car looking like zombies—or worse from a dog's perspective—a veterinarian.

Barking, growling, lunging with his lips curled back and leaping up and down and spinning around like a swordfish inside the cruiser— from back seat to front seat and back again— racing in circles in an attempt to cover every window.

The dog was intent on beating back every one of the assailants.

Smokey was off the chart fierce and frantic.

And Red, who never did have the kind of control over the dog one would like to see, is now in no shape to be handling the mutt.

Red's lost quite a bit of blood. He's in pain and in shock.

Even if the injured warden can muster the strength to talk tough to the 100 pound dog and swing his stick at the beast, it's not enough to convince the dog to let these strangers walk up and carry his master out of the cruiser.

Smokey is sensitive enough to know his boss was in bad shape—certainly the dog smelled blood.

The dog musta figured these people coming at the car intended to hurt the old man even more.

The dog played the only card he always did—let these folks know he would tear them to pieces before they touched the boss.

For more than 10 minutes, doctors and nurses tried various approaches to get past Smokey and to Red.

They had half of the crew drop back 10 feet, then 40 feet, while one brave soul tries to sneak up on Smokey.

Then they try a diversion.

One person heads towards the trunk to get Smokey to jump in the back seat and focus on them while another tries the get low and walk like a duck, intending to make a dive for the driver's door, pull Red out and slam it fast.

But Smokey ain't no dummy.

He's not fooled by any of this and he's a pro at leaping from the front seat to the back seat and back again.

All the time this is going on, Red is yelling at the dog "By the Judas Priest" and worse, and swinging his stick—but certainly not with his usual vigor and to no effect whatsoever.

The Dispatcher is trying to communicate with Red, too. But no one can hear anything back at base except Smokey's roar.

The medical team drops back into a huddle and weighs their choices:

A) get one or more people bit badly trying to

subdue the dog while others grab Red;

B) find someone to subdue—as in dart or shoot and kill—the dog;

C) find someone the dog knows and trusts to calm the maniac mutt down and remove him from the cruiser, so the medical team can attend to Red.

Wisely, no one chooses option A—just open up the car door and wrestle with Smokey.

As for option B, if anyone was capable of shooting Smokey to stop this one dog brawl it would be Red.

But he's not reaching for his Colt and it would be a big mistake to think he would let anyone else do it, even if it meant Red bleeding to death.

That left "C."

Some of the staff know Rocky Hooper, Red's son.

Over his lifetime, Rocky worked for the town of Johnson in a variety of roles: health officer, road crew, Select Board member and even police chief.

Folks think maybe Rocky can handle his dad's dog.

A nurse runs into the hospital and gets on a phone and calls the Johnson Town Offices. As quickly as she can, she explains the situation.

Can they get ahold of Rocky and have him drive
on over from Johnson to Copley and get the dog
out of the cruiser so the doctors and nurses can
help his father?

It's now been well more than an hour since the
bullet blasted into the old man's thigh.

Who exactly reached Rocky, I don't know.
But Rocky gets the message and rushes over
to Copley.

Lucky for Red, Rocky drives faster than his
dad, and he's also an animal lover. Rocky pulls
his work truck up alongside Red's cruiser and
jumps out with a leash in one hand and a dog
biscuit in the other—all in under 15 minutes.

Rocky raises his hand and waves at the nurses
and doctors with a pushing motion, telling them
to get back farther.

The dog sees Rocky and sees that the strangers
are backing away.

Smokey starts wagging his tail and quiets down,
happy a familiar face has arrived.

He's exhausted from having to fend off all these
people alone, protecting Red.

Red rolls down his window a little to speak
to his son.

Rocky leans in. "How you doin', Dad?"
he asks.

"Been better," Red chuckles. "Thanks for
coming. Smokey doesn't like all this fuss."

Smokey's nose is already out the rear window,
trying to lick Rocky's hand.

"I'll take Smokey home, Dad," Rocky says.
"Then I'll come right back."

Rocky waits until the medical team is safe
inside the sliding glass doors of the hospital.

He doesn't want to give Smokey any reason to
get all stirred up again.

He shows Smokey the dog biscuit and pops open
the back door just wide enough to feed Smokey
the treat.

As the big dog begins to munch, Rocky snaps
the lead onto the dog's collar.

Then Rocky opens the passenger door to his
truck and encourages Smokey to jump in, which
the dog does immediately.

Rocky follows, shuts the truck door and looks
over towards the emergency room door to give
the doctors and nurses a thumbs up, allowing
them to charge in to save Red.

Red spends two weeks in the hospital.

His room fills with cards and flowers.

He hates the fuss, asks about Smokey several times a day and is itchin' to get out of there.

When Red arrives home, he finds more Get Well cards waiting for him, along with many homemade casseroles, pies and breads—and one pretty gift box with a fancy red bow.

Inside is a shiny new leather holster.

No card.

"Red turned and walked with tenderness up the Long Trail—reaching out to brace himself on the bark of this tree and then reaching out to another—the old dog zig zagging at his heels."

REMEMBERIN' RED
T'OTHER SIDE

CONTRIBUTED BY RICHARD HISLOP

During my few months with Red, he was laid low by some bug that kept him off the road about a week.

He'd pulled through. But age takes a toll on healing and time spent flat on your back—helpless as a newborn pup—makes you appreciate all you stand to lose.

Red was past the age when most folks retire. And his weren't no desk job. This is a fellow who worked hard.

More than ever, I was intent on making certain my mentor stayed healthy while I was riding shotgun.

But Red didn't make that easy.

About a week after he was back on his feet, Red pulled up near the Long Trail at Laraway Mountain, threw the cruiser into park and surprised me with a little announcement.

He looked at the trail sign and said nonchalantly, "Smokey and I are going to take a little walk over the mountain," and opened the driver's door.

He climbed out with some effort and opened the back door for Smokey to step out alongside him. Both man and dog moved deliberately, gingerly to protect their arthritic joints.

I jumped out of the driver's door, trying to think of a polite way to stop Red.

Flashes of Babe's anger raced into my head and how I had dodged disaster that day.

Now, here I am a little older and a lot wiser, but if I let Red go off alone and anything happened to him, I'd never hear the end of it.

All these ideas and more are slamming around in my brain like a pinball machine.

Let anything happen to Red and I'd be lucky to get a job flipping burgers at an all night diner.

And more than that, I really liked and respected the man. I'd feel awful.

So, I leaned over the top of the cruiser and in as nonchalant a tone as I could muster, I said, "Uh Red, you sure you want to do that?"

Red ignored me. He was reaching into the back seat of the cruiser and stuffing a couple odds and ends in his pockets.

When he was done, he straightened his back with a bit of effort and looked at me over the top of the car.

"A-yuh. We're goin," he says, reaching down to give Smokey a pat on the head.

"I think I should come along with you," I say as tactfully as I can.

Red lowers his head and looks over the top of his glasses at me.

"I know what you've been told," he said, pausing and squirming a little. It was too uncomfortable for Red to say out loud, "I know you're not supposed to let me be alone."

His voice had a touch of sadness in it.

I didn't respond.

I wasn't surprised at some level that Red knew it. This guy had sources the FBI would envy. But I sure wish he didn't know, you know?

Red turned his head and looked behind him at the trail sign and the steep climb and then turned back to me.

"It's like this. I don't know how much longer Smokey and I will be able to climb this mountain," he said. "But today, I know we can. So, we're going," he said with a steely glint in his eyes. "And we're going alone."

I looked at Red and saw a longing for understanding from a man less than half his age. He knew and I knew if I really wanted to stop him, I could.

I was young, strong and fit. No question I could stop him from setting foot on the trail.

And I knew that bothered him, too—as it would any man who prided himself on being rugged.

Because not so many years ago, no one would have had the upper hand on Red Hooper in a fight—not in a fistfight, not in a shoot out.

For that matter, he'd best most anyone in a battle of wits too—still could. But all the years of hard work had taken a toll.

I looked down at Smokey, his muzzle shot through with white hair and his coat coarse and a little dull with age. I had no doubt his teeth were still sharp enough to take someone down, it would just take him longer to catch 'em, too.

I felt a kind of guilt—I had something Red didn't have anymore: youth.

But it wasn't me that was running out the clock on Red. It was Father Time that was the thief.

I stood there in awkward silence trying to decide what to do. Red saw by the look on my face I was squirming inside and he spoke up. "We'll be fine. You just drive over t'other side

and we'll meet you at Ober Hill in about four
hours," he said.

I was calculating how far the hike was. About
nine miles and pretty steep going at times. A
lot of kids couldn't do it, let alone a man his age
who'd been very ill.

I weigh my choices: I can try and talk him out
of it. I can physically restrain him. I can radio
for help. I can follow him. I can just let him go.

This is a tough one. I feel like I've got battery
acid in my stomach.

I take a deep breath, swallow hard, look down at
my boots and when I raise my head, I make sure
I've pasted a smile on my face. I don't want him
to see how concerned I am.

"Okay, Red. I'll meet you over on the other side,"
I say. Like it was no big deal.

Like my career and the rest of my life doesn't
hinge on the old man making it over the
mountain alive and in good shape.

I let him go, because I realized I'd want some
young upstart to do the same for me—just leave
me alone to enjoy one of my last walks in the
woods with my dog.

Red turned and walked with tenderness up the
Long Trail—reaching out to brace himself on
the bark of this tree and then reaching out to
another—the old dog zig zagging at his heels.

293

They disappeared out of sight in less than a minute.

I kick some dirt, pick a few stems of sweet
grass growing beside the road, chew on 'em.
I'm standing quietly and listening hard.

I wait at the trailhead a good hour, just in case
Red changes his mind and yells for me, fires his
weapon or Smokey comes back alone. When
I'm pretty certain neither Red nor Smokey will
be coming back down the trail, I start the drive
around the mountain.

I stop at a few fishing holes along the way to
check anglers' licenses, to keep myself occupied
and earn my salary. But I find myself checking
my watch every few minutes.

When I can't stand it any longer, I get back in
the cruiser and pull in at Ober Hill, get out and
stand at the end of the trail and listen.

When Red and Smokey step out of the woods, I feel
like I'd been holding my breath for about five hours.

I don't make a fuss or congratulate Red or
Smokey on making the journey. I didn't want
Red to think I thought he might not make it.

Smokey's tongue is about dragging on the ground
and he looks like his hips are bothering him. I
open the back door of the cruiser and the dog
crawls in. He's out like a light within two minutes.

"How about I drive us home?" I say to Red.

He doesn't argue.

Red slides into the passenger seat—tired but quietly triumphant. Unlike a lot of guys, he doesn't share what he'd seen on his hike or brag on the fact he and his old dog had made the hike despite their ailments.

That wasn't Red.

Years have passed. Looking back on that day, it strikes me that what I said to Red—about meeting him on the other side—it kinda has a second, deeper meaning.

I sure do hope to meet up with Red—and a lot of other first rate fellows who wore the badge—on the other side of the mountain one day.

Because there's not much better in Life—or in the Hereafter either, to my way of thinking about it—than sitting around a campfire swapping stories of good men, good dogs and our wild adventures.

But if Someone's listening, I'm in no hurry.

Acknowledgements

This book could not have been completed without the encouragement and skill of the following individuals:

**Jean McHenry, Sandy Brisson,
Carrie Cook, Bob Lutz,
Al and Karen Myers,
Norma Montaigne, Mary Wing,
Debra Russell Sanborn,
Dorrice and John Hammer,
W. Douglas Darby, Paul A. Young,
Stephen P. Frost, Jean Cross,
Inge Schaefer, Sam Stanley,
Joanne and Fred Doucette,
Eric and Ingrid Nuse,
Art Chase, Henry Giddings,
Richard Fifield, Tom Simpson,
Patsy Munson, Tammy Walker,
Anne Bugbee and O.C.**

Thank you, one and all.

Many thanks to the following wardens...

 **John Kapusta** worked 38 years as a Vermont warden. John resides in Hardwick, VT.

 **Richard Hislop** worked 34 years as a Vermont warden. Richard resides in Fairfax, VT.

 **Wayne Rowell** worked 32 years as a Vermont warden. Wayne resides in Wilmington, VT.

 **Robert Rooks** worked 29 years as a Vermont warden. Robert resides in Westford, VT.

 **Stan Holmquist** worked 27 years as a Vermont warden. Stan resides in Rochester, VT.

...FOR ALLOWING ME TO SHARE THEIR STORIES

 **Bob Lutz** worked 23 years as a Vermont warden. Bob resides in Fairfax, VT

 **Denny Gaiotti** worked 29 years as a Vermont warden. Denny resides in Whiting, VT.

 **Eric Nuse** worked 32 years as a Vermont warden. Eric resides in Johnson, VT.

 **Tom Stearns** worked 32 years as a Vermont warden. Tom is now a resident of South Dakota and travels the nation in his RV.

STORIES BY WARDEN

John Kapusta
TRAIL BLAZER, EVEL ENVY, CREAM PUFF
SNOW BRAWL, COUGAR, MEASURE OF A MAN

Richard Hislop
DON'T LOSE HIM, PESKY PAYCHECKS
EYES IN THE FOREST, BOY SCOUT MANNERS
SHOT FIRED, T'OTHER SIDE

Wayne Rowell
FULL HOUSE, STRAIGHT FLUSH, WEAR AND TEAR

Robert Rooks
CHUCK CHASE, MONKEY MUDDLE

Stan Holmquist
KEEPIN' UP WITH THE JONESES

Bob Lutz
KNIFEMAN

Denny Gaiotti
HOTSHOT

Eric Nuse
HITCHHIKER

Tom Stearns
SNOWMAN

Who We Are

Megan Price is a former award winning journalist and Vermont legislator. She enjoys turning good stories into great books.

Bob Lutz is a talented caricaturist, creating quirky illustrations. Bob lives in Fairfax, VT.

Carrie Cook is an exceptional graphic designer and musician who lives in Cambridge, VT.

Norma Montaigne served as a consultant on this book and owns Anything Graphic in Pittsford, VT.

Want more great stories?

Buy Volumes One & Two!

Visit

www.VermontWild.com